Boundless Mercy

Boundless Mercy

Markus Ray

Immortal Ray Productions

Nashville   Washington D.C.

"Om, I bow to Her Who is full

of Boundless Mercy."

—Sri Shastriji—

IMMORTAL RAY PRODUCTIONS
301 TINGEY STREET SE, #338
WASHINGTON DC, 20003

immortalrayproductions@gmail.com

Immortal Ray Productions

Nashville Washington D.C.

Library of Congress Cataloging in Publication Data

Ray, Markus; Boundless Mercy

1. Prose-Poetry. 2. Meditations. 3. Life Wisdom

Cover Design: Immortal Ray Productions
Cover Image: Judy Totton Photography of London
Back Cover Image: Immortal Ray Productions

ISBN 13: Paperback 978-1-950684-10-6
ISBN 13: E-Book 978-1-950684-11-3

Other Books by Markus Ray

❈ Miracles with My Master, Tara Singh

❈ Odes to the Divine Mother

❈ Little Ganesh Book

❈ The Master Is Beautiful

❈ Alpha Omega

❈ The Second Coming

Co-Authored with Sondra Ray

❈ Spiritual Intimacy

❈ Babaji: My Miraculous Meetings
with a Maha Avatar

❈ Liberation: Freedom from Your Biggest
Block to Pure Joy

❈ Physical Immortality: How to Overcome
Death

Table of Contents

Boundless Mercy

The Great Sequester Begins

Dedication

I dedicate this book to Sondra Ray, my Queen and Consort. She is the Muse of my Inspiration. Where she goes do I go. What she feels do I feel. What she sees do I see. The Divine Mother touches her deeply, and through her am I touched with the grace of the Divine Mother as well, and by all of the Spiritual Masters who fulfill my every need with Boundless Mercy.

Markus Ray

Washington DC
December 1, 2020

Foreword

In October, Markus Ray and I had a brief email exchange about whether he should put his then 200+ handwritten daily writings about "boundless mercy" out there. I jokingly asked him if he ever had any **bad** ideas? The answer is no.

Then I asked if I could transcribe for him. I had already done *Odes to the Divine Mother* and the *Little Ganesh Book*, so I was familiar with the content of his heart and his handwriting in his beautiful Italian leather journals. The answer was yes, and he suggested I title the pages if I wanted to. I did.

In my long association with Markus as client (I am a copy editor) and friend, I have been influenced by his expression and his example of right living. He has a way with words and is an influencer of the most-meaningful kind. Yes, he has his social media followers, and his art lover followers—he is an artist and poet as well. He has been around the world numerous times with his wife Sondra Ray teaching loving relationships, joy, peace, beauty, forgiveness, truth, and miracles. What he wants to show and tell us is that these are not abstract, no-longer-applicable, other-worldly ideals belonging only to saints and sages. They are the everyday real stuff we are made of in addition to blood and bone, and they are around us in everything, everywhere, all the time if we will only see. This is what Markus writes about.

He is the ultimate observer, knowing that what he sees outside us is within us; all connected and all in good order. He writes in longhand because he likes the feel of pen in hand, the sound of scratch on a page—not because he is not tech savvy (he is, as you will see) and not for the sake of being sentimental or romantic, but because it is about connection. All his looking, deep listening, and writing is an act of connecting authentically with himself and his surrounds, and in doing so, connecting with all of us. We are not islands. We are not isolated even in this time of a world pandemic when it feels like it. We are one, together, in humanity. Markus takes us around the world with him and proves this on every page.

I was happy to join him in some familiar places. I transcribed his pages mostly between 3 and 5:30 a.m. before husband and dogs got up and the day demanded another kind of attention. These are sacred hours in which I am rested and open to give and receive the highest honor of attention and understanding to what is before me. The wisdom of these pages was my sole morning meditation for many weeks. When I arose from the keyboard, I was fed and fueled, loved, seen, forgiven, connected to the boundless mercy surrounding us all, and thankful.

—Barbara Milbourn—
Nashville, Tennessee

Boundless Mercy

Boundless Mercy

I am writing a book called Boundless Mercy because that is what most of us need. That is what the world needs as well. It is obvious. Never have there been greater means available to the human race to destroy itself; and never have there been greater means available for us to connect ourselves through social media and fluency of communication to realize the Oneness, Wholeness, and Innocence that we really are. Each of you reading this introduction must choose. "You are the world," as the great sage Krishnamurti said. The conflicts and strife that are observable in the world are mere amplifications and manifestations of the conflicts and strife in us. You and I are more the same than different. The collective consciousness of humanity forms a unified field. These are facts. Our own personal trials and conflicts added together 7.8 billion times makes up the world. But each of us in this 7.8 billion-member human race has the capacity for higher thoughts of liberation from conflict and strife. This capacity is collective as well. Added together 7.8 billion times, one kind thought of self-forgiveness could change our world, and usher in a new age of Boundless Mercy.

2

Extreme Pardon

Mercy is extreme pardon. It is like saying, "Your past does not matter. It has no real consequences now." Mercy is a correction, not a punishment. Punishment is never justified in the eyes of Mercy. Therefore, there is no attack in it, no violence. It is an absolution of debt. This does not mean that the debt is left unpaid, but it brings forgiveness to the paying of the debt. What does this really mean in the end—freedom from guilt? Guilt is never justified. Innocence as a human being is his or her original birth-right. To owe money is to have a debt. But this does not make the person who owes the money guilty. Most people who own a home pay a mortgage to a bank. This debt does not make them guilty, even though they understand the debt has to be paid. Debt in this case is like a contract, an agreement, a binding rule that two parties enter into. Soul contracts are similar. We agree to be with some people in this life to learn to be merciful. Maybe we were not in the past. Maybe we owed them a debt unpaid. The one who is "owed" the debt as well as the one who is paying off the debt have a responsibility to complete the transaction. The ultimate mercy is to "forgive the debt." If the one who is "owed" forgives the debtor, that is an act of Boundless Mercy.

3

A Different Reality

The fear that grips our thought about the future nags at our mind regardless of the situation. In a plethora of abundance, one wonders when the next drought of dearth will sweep across the plains of our fertile fate, turning the golden grains of a plentiful harvest into the dried-up stalks of a sunburnt crop of despair. We are sort of in this moment of uncertainty all the time, with a nagging inkling of "what if," bringing a doldrum to our days. All the more reason Mercy is needed. The human brain seems wired for doubt and destruction with a shelf life of seventy or eighty years before the decline of reason takes hold and moves us toward an "inevitable death." The inherent fear of this dynamic makes us uneasy. Some kind of a battle with ourselves ensues. Pains are felt, as are joys, and they vie for ascendency. Maintaining a constant joy seems challenging in this state of future concern. We do not go gently into that dark night, nor do we feel consoled by a God who made up the rules for engagement in this mortal life. "There must be another way," we rightly think, to give us an option here. What loving God would leave us in the lurch? What fear of death would not be challenged by a Creator who cares for the Created? No more would fear hold sway over the mind that sees a different realty. World without end is promised to those who have a different vision of Truth. What lack goes on in the advent of Boundless Mercy?

4

A New Way

We are trapped in a prison of thought, it seems, with the bars of beliefs we keep thinking. As creatures of habit we fall in the ruts of our repetitive behaviors, even if they are not good for us. Mistakes can be made again and again. Then an epiphany may jolt us to change. We adopt a new way of thinking. We must, or we get the repeated results that led us over and over again to the same discontent. The mind is full of loops and winding wheels and treadmills of thoughts. We are conditioned to seek advantage yet may end up filling our days with wasted motions, spinning these wheels but going nowhere. What is the certain path to happiness and bliss? What engulfs our mind and soul with the frequency of freedom, peace, and joy? There are moments when the old habits just won't do—they are seen as the very prison house from which we must escape. We have had ample time to ponder our inner world in this Great Sequester. What could have been a complete shutdown in our work around the globe became the opener of a new way of Life. Self-reliance became more meaningful in communicating across oceans and continents and ethernets. We began a new way of working, building on the firm foundation of twelve years of global travel behind us. I wrote to a man in prison who read my *Little Ganesh Book*. Somehow the relationships meant to be are furthered in these times of Boundless Mercy.

5

The Key that Opens

Prisons could be a place where mistakes are forgiven, not "punished." Misguided people who committed crimes suffer from lack of love and have had no mercy. They have become tough and ruthless, angry, and isolated in their quest for self-survival. Society has placed them in quarantine, set apart from the whole in order to prevent them from doing more "harm" to themselves and others. Crime is associated with punishment. We give prisons fancy names like "houses of correction," yet they are permeated with the "guilt" of the separated self. Separated from love, the balancing of the scale of justice boils down to the old law of an eye for an eye and a tooth for a tooth. You must pay your debt with suffering. Guilt demands punishment. The two are bound to one another in the human psyche. Memories of guilt, crime, and punishment are perpetuated. We are all subject to this mental dynamic. The prison house of guilt is in our mind and is the culprit of fear. Fear makes us do things that may not be the best for the whole. Self-centered in the ego of "me," the human being is isolated from his neighbors and from his true Self. This isolation brings about anxiety, anger, pressure of survival, selfish acts of disregard. The prison house of separation from love is what we all need to escape. Forgiveness is the key that opens the iron gates of guilt and allows us to walk out freely into the absolution of Boundless Mercy.

6

The Heart of the Matter

I got a post on my Facebook today from my friend Sage Stewart from Colorado. It was a picture of a heart drawn on a sidewalk with chalk, and inside the rainbow-colored heart it read "Love is here." His caption read, "Remember a tool is only as good as the person who uses it—The Heart." This is true in the world of good craft. I have been a craftsman for many years, perhaps lifetimes, and I learned that good tools are a must, but good craft is even more a must—and good tools do not necessarily produce a good craftsman. In the hands of a novice, a Stradivarius would just produce noise, but in the hands of Yo-Yo Ma, the same instrument can utter heavenly music. I worked in the building trades and always bought myself the best equipment and the best materials, yet I know it was only my commitment to precision, integrity, and inner correction that made the final construction "good craft." My next-door neighbor, Uncle Lenny, worked in the trades as well. He was one of the worst craftsmen I ever met. If a board was cut too small, he would say, "just caulk it." If something would go wrong on a job, he would blame it on Murphy's Law. Whatever could go wrong would go wrong, according to Uncle Lenny. I loved him anyway. He would help me on my jobs, but I would only trust him with demolition. He did that very well. A good demolisher he was. In the end, Love does not care if the other does not use the tools well. God does not care if we screw up. Love is based on Boundless Mercy.

7

The Unknown and the Teacher

Love is mostly abiding in the Unknown. We live in the world of the known, and that is the past. Love, like God, is beyond our understanding. It is in the present, but we are abiding in the past with what we have stored as memory. The conglomerate of memories is the known. It is a recorded impression of the past we have stored up and experienced. Yet we live in the present. What we are experiencing, though, is affected by the memories of the past until we become aware of this tendency. We become comfortable with the familiar. We need these memories to function, yet there is a space in the present free of memory. This Unknown space is very energetic, very still, and very silent. It pervades everything in the Universe. It is Love; it is Truth; it is non-physical; yet it permeates everything physical. It exists even before thought. My teacher, Tara Singh, wrote a book called "The Voice that Precedes Thought." This is not a Voice that we are accustomed to speaking, because we use thought so much, we seldom reduce our mind down to this point of original precedence. To do that we must embrace the Unknown, and the Unknown is scary, so we avoid it. This has very startling implications: we live in a state of low-level fear much of the time. It is suppressed yet underlying thought itself. To step out of thought requires a teacher who has already done it. This is a great gift of life to meet such a person who lives in the realm of Boundless Mercy.

8

Choosing in the Now

Memory contains impressions, recollections of the past. A "hard drive" of the mind, it collects these impressions of the continuous moments of Now. The quality of one's experience of the present, the Now, affects memory and fills it with this quality. What one "knows" is also colored by this quality of the Now. Right Now, I am experiencing an impression of delight, of joy, of fulfillment in this moment of writing. The beauty of this book, the cream-colored paper, the amazing invention of this pen, the leather cover of this book made in Italy, the music playing on the iPod in the background, the cool air of early autumn—all combine in this present moment of Love. Love is clearly in the present and is experienced there. At the same time, I could acknowledge the role of memory. Without it I would not "know" how to write down these impressions. I would need a language to express my Joy. This "medium" has been developed over eons of time. English has taken thousands of years to develop, as all other languages have as well. But the medium is not the message. The message is what is going on in the communicator right now. The medium of the past, the known, delivers the quality of the Unknown, the present, in this moment of joy, of Love. In this way we can put into our memory the joys of Love or the sorrows of pain. It is always our decision to make. In the midst of present difficulties, we can still choose joy instead of sorrow—this choice is Boundless Mercy.

9

Meritorious of Mercy

I have developed a style of writing in which I explore a train of thought for one page. I am good for one page and most readers in this age want something short and to the point. This style began with writing poetry and got perfected with *Odes to the Divine Mother*. Now the subject is Boundless Mercy. These are words, like God, like Love, which are so far beyond verbal description. "Catch a falling star and put it in your pocket; save it for a rainy day." This was the theme of a song from my childhood. Mercy of the boundless variety is as elusive as a falling star. Yet, because it is beyond the realm of our thinking, a different state of mind is necessary to make contact with it. All the things that are not working in your life must be put on the table. A kind of confession invokes another energy of self-honesty in which all issues are exposed. The mind is now open and vulnerable for correction from a dimension beyond thought, beyond memory stored up in the brain. In this state of mind, the innocence of who You are as God created you comes forth. This Self-Identity is meritorious of mercy. Because there is willingness to see mistakes and to correct them, and to take 100 percent responsibility for all issues, this invokes the help of Higher Forces. The power of this help is unfathomable. It invites the boon of Boundless Mercy.

10

Song of the Day

A song of the day begins with deep listening. In this form of listening there is no judgment and no motive. The song takes shape in the sounds that are given. As soon as I arise, my consort and I make the bed in a beautiful way. We pull up the sheets and the blankets, smooth out any wrinkles, place the pillows and fold them under the covers, arrange the brightly embroidered Indian cloth over the bed spread, and admire the beauty of the whole thing. This is the first melody in the song of our day. It is a happy note of togetherness. Then we proceed to take our showers. In our apartment there is a men's bath and women's bath, so we each have our own unique space for this morning ritual. In the men's bath there are pictures of men who have sung a song of enlightenment to humanity. Some would be familiar faces: Lincoln, Jesus, Emerson, Thoreau, and Whitman. Others from the East are Krishnamurti, Tara Singh, Vivekananda, Ramakrishna. And in more recent times Babaji and Muniraj. These are all men of virtue. They had something of Truth, of God, to impart to humanity. Their words remain here with us, and the story of their deeds inspire us to our own greatness. Their presence in the men's bath compose the next melody in the song of my day. And the one who sings the loudest is the one the most silent—Sri Ramana Maharshi, the sage of Arunachala. He spoke very little, but when he did people were liberated in his presence. His face is a song of Boundless Mercy.

11

This Extension of Everything

Who reads for the purpose of inner transformation? Who writes to awaken himself to a new truth and in so doing gives an opening in the mind of his readers? And about what? It is hardly conceivable to write a whole book on the subject of two words—Boundless Mercy. The undertaking itself is an action of Boundless Mercy. What would I say about it that is my direct insight and experience? Start where you are with what you have. This is such an all-pervasive subject; you can find it anywhere. Anything "boundless" permeates the very air we breathe. It is in the pen and paper, in the countertop, in the light that illuminates the day, and in the shadows that are inevitably cast in the process of observing this extension of everything. Any physical thing has an edge. A particular entity has a body. It could be an atom, a particle, or a planet. Size does not matter. Yet anything in a body has two major qualities: it is contained within its structural integrity (which is limited in its particular form, therefore not boundless), and it is related and part of a whole cosmos (which is unlimited and boundless). Even science is not certain "how big" the cosmos extends. It may not even have an edge, an "end." In which case, it is boundless. As humans, we have the same two qualities. We have a body and a mind—limited to the conditions of memory; and we have a spirit which is not limited to any confines. To place our awareness on the unlimited nature of our Self, the Whole, is an act of Boundless Mercy.

12

Action that Transcends Definition

One page a day. A discipline forces the mind to go deeper into the subject of Boundless Mercy. Unexpected responses flood into the mind by the sheer will of attention. When I think of something "boundless" my mind enters a cosmic space. It makes contact with the Unknown. In my little world there can be resistance to face this Unknown. Immobilized by the fear of a label— stupid, uninformed, insignificant—my mind fills the empty space with all kinds of inventions and projections. Boundless Mercy defines itself in an action that transcends definition. It meets the needs of those who have needs. Necessity is the main invocation of this form of divine providence. Writing a whole book on these two words scares my mind into its lowest doubts. Looking in the beginning of this book and seeing a few hundred pages ahead—the blank pages of the great Unknown—brings to the surface a whole flood of uncertainty to face. Does a flower have a motive? Being colorful and fragrant is its nature, effortlessly extending itself in the whole flow of cosmic occurrences. As it blooms, a flare on the sun's surface shoots out, simultaneously. Birds fly overhead. The washing machine spins its rinse cycle. I can hear the flip-flop of my wife's slip-on shoes as she walks across the kitchen. The squirrel looks for an acorn in the park lawns under the oak tree. All things happen at once. I am not aware of all the particular occurrences in the universe, yet the wondrous fact that they are occurring is Boundless Mercy in action.

13

Words

The word and the actuality of the word is the subject. Lofty words like love, truth, gratitude, trust, must be practiced in order to be realized. We soon discover our inconsistencies in applying these words. A person we loved in the past is no longer loved in the present. Time changes our perspective; an absolute word is brought down to the time level and stripped of its true meaning. Certain words are absolute, changeless, unlimited—and we turn them into relative words, changeable, limited. "I love you, but . . ." It is the "but" which makes the word relative and conditional, giving us an "out" in our application. Therefore, discovering the absolute quality of the word evades us. We would have to confront our inconsistencies and undo them in order to make contact with the actuality of the word. The word is not the "thing." The word "apple" is not the apple. The word Love is not Love. Love is a changeless state of pure joy and connection beyond the conditions of thought. The great sages and saints abide in the actuality of this word: Love. They have realized Love as an action of giving, of pure creation, of perfect alignment with the cosmic forces of life. There is consistency in their words, deeds, and actions, at all levels of their being. Love is free of conflict, fear, attack, judgment, discontent. The application of an Absolute word takes one's whole life. In many cases, we fail, and this is why forgiveness is necessary to invoke the grace of Boundless Mercy.

14

Sunday is a Good Day

On Sunday, rest and leisure put one closer to the Divine mind. The tasks of the week are put aside. Naturally, a day of introspection, Sunday is given to God. One seventh of Life, focused on disengaging from activity, provides an opportunity for new possibilities to emerge. One develops a relationship to the Unknown. In this spacious emptiness Love can enter awareness because our attention is not taken up with "doing things." In this space of openness new encounters happen in the most surprising way. A stranger comes into your midst. After a few lines of conversation, he is no longer "strange." He could turn into a friend for life. Or perhaps you meet someone for a few seconds or minutes, and never meet them again in this lifetime. Sunday is an energy of contemplation. Part of everyday benefits from being a little piece of Sunday. One ponders the greater meaning of Life: Why am I here? What is my purpose? What is my life's mission? What do I need to change in myself for my mission to fully manifest? What is my next action? These are the questions of an introspective life. They are also the catalyst for Action. Life is Action. Movement. Manifestation. What is your destiny to make manifest? Sunday is a good day to think about these important questions, which contain the pure energy of growth, change, and fulfillment. The questions are more important than verbal answers. They are questions that can only be answered with the overall Action of one's whole life. Yet, in the midst of living the answer, a person needs the unknown guidance of Boundless Mercy.

15

Divine Leisure

Divine Leisure abides in the natural tendency to do what you like to do. It creates from a space inside which is natural and intrinsic. This nature produces something inevitable—like an apple tree is destined to produce apples. A writer is predisposed to write; a painter to paint. Some things are learned, yet other talents and tendencies are already present, not acquired over time. The expression of this talent or gift has its natural flow. An apple tree yields its apples in the fall season. A human, in the same regard, has his or her season for being fruitful. This is an effortless extension of Divine Leisure. My Life Teacher, Tara Singh, often spoke of Divine Leisure as the natural state of the human being. In fact, it is the function of the human being on earth to make contact with the Divine Reality of the cosmos, and this awareness is his or her main contribution in Life. If we are not in touch with this actual divine and cosmic connection, then we are caught in lower levels of survival of the body, the ego of the personality, and various other emotional entanglements. Divine Leisure enables the human being to step out of these more common concerns. By doing so, he or she enters into the higher realm of a spiritual life, a life connected to higher laws, truths, and principles. The highest law is Love, of course, but it takes a whole Life of devotion to Divine Leisure to plumb the depths of this Absolute reality. For this reason, the wholeness of Life in our awareness requires the grace of Boundless Mercy.

16

Rainy Days and Relationships

A rainy day pervades my mind, and naturally I seek shelter in the introspective recesses which provide the hearth in which I may light some new fire to dry and warm my dampened soul. Gratitude is the sure fire that burns away the doldrums. My biggest gratitude is to God for providing my relationship with Sondra Ray. Her influence in my life, along with Tara Singh, has been the most profound. She introduced me to A Course in Miracles, and Tara Singh completed that destiny for me. These two relationships, along with those from our India travels, have filled my life with wisdom and joy. Everyone can probably acknowledge a couple key relationships in their life that have been transformative. They may even have altered the course of your destiny or been the most important components that shaped your life. On any gray and rainy day, they provide the brightness which can lift you out of the shadows of discontent into the new illumination of a cheerful day. These key relationships have inspired you to go to the heights of your own being. One could be related to a writer from the past through books. My first encounter with Henry David Thoreau made him my friend for life. I read passages from *Walden* which uplifted me beyond measure; there were also passages which turned my world upside down and required I examine my life with new eyes. Thoreau can cut away the misconceptions and conditions in your mind, and on a rainy day, provide Boundless Mercy.

17

The Quality of Attitude

Every morning holds out the new possibilities of realizing Pure Joy. We can listen to the songs of a happy day within ourselves or to the complaints of discontent. There may be challenges, work tasks, obstacles to overcome, yet the attitude of gratitude helps one face these challenges with the clarity of action that solves all problems. Hymns of praise are far more productive than the cacophony of criticism. Acknowledgment is the honey of good relationships. For those of us who hold ourselves to a high standard of excellence, it is important to acknowledge ourselves as well, and give more attention to our victories than to our defeats. Winning is more often than not learning what not to do again. After many failed attempts to invent the incandescent light bulb, Edison declared in a logically positive way, "I have discovered 200 ways how not to do it." And each small failure then became the necessary steppingstone to final victory and truly new discovery. Had discouragement taken Edison over in the most critical hours of a breakthrough, we may still be groping around with a candle in the dark. When one loves the journey as much as the arrival at the final destination, all the "wrong turns" and unexpected vistas on the long and winding scenic route become the joyful song of an independent life. You are the master of your own destiny. Where you are going is not merely as important as the quality of attitude in getting there. This attitude of gratitude paves the way for new discovery and opens the door to certain victory. Then, even in defeat, are the joys of Boundless Mercy.

18

Our Thoughts

We seem to be victims—at the effects—of past thoughts and memories of traumas. The pains of the past haunt us and tend to repeat themselves in different forms. We have scars, battle wounds that linger and remind us of incidents best forgotten. Yet the scar is also useful to help us forgive as well and release the thought we had which caused the traumatic effects in the first place. We are never victims of the past, nor of the traumatic memories, nor of the negative thought forms which we can transmute and change. We rule our minds and have sovereignty over our thoughts. That means we choose the thoughts we think. Even if they seem to be someone else's thoughts, or our family's thoughts, or our society's thoughts, we allow them, or not, to have dominion in our minds. We can just as easily think lofty thoughts with God in the present. The thoughts we think with God are only joyful. Or they are a correction of our thoughts that are not joyful. A simple observation could be full of joyful thoughts—a fall dusk observed from the picture window of a coffee shop reveals an intense light that casts long shadows of the passersby as they stroll down the sidewalk. The gentle breeze blows the hair of the blonde collegiate woman, catching the backlit rays of the setting sun like a filter of brilliant beatitudes to the natural elements that bless our days. Only a moment in the overture of this one-page composition, yet a note that sounds eternal. All these thoughts we think with God well up from the stillness of Boundless Mercy.

19

In Times of Loss

There are memories of loss. My teacher died. Then my marriage was over. My father died. Then my mother died. Never such grief had I experienced than when my mother, alone and confused in an old-people's home, yearned to be taken home to be with her children, and I was not able to fulfill that wish. By then I was with the love of my life, Sondra Ray, but even that love could not prevent me from feeling the incredible grief of the situation with my mother. When she passed a month and 26 days after her 90th birthday, I was almost relieved that her confusion and misery of aloneness was over. I was in her hospital room when she passed. By the time I arrived she was in a coma, yet I had some hours by her side, holding her hand. I took a short nap, and the nurse woke me when she had passed. I had the nurses dress her in some of her better clothes then I paid my respects and left after a final goodbye. Back at my sister's house, I got a few hours of rest. Not much to say. In the morning I made my flight arrangements back to Nashville, and within a few hours was on a plane back home. There is a shock that comes with death. For a spell, the mind is wiped clean of concerns in a kind of suspended animation. One is still moving in the world, yet one's thought is disengaged, detached, not a participant as much as it is merely a witness. The witnessing of a death of a parent is one of the more profound experiences of my life. Death is within Life. In this time is when one is closest to Boundless Mercy.

20

In Quest of the Self

We are all on a quest to discover our Self. This Self is immortal, unlimited, and Absolute. Yet we seek the Self in contrast to the mortal, limited, and relative self we are constantly trying to perfect and improve. The self of the personality, with all its fears, faults, and character "defects," seems to be the predominant focus of our attention. The quest to awaken and live in our Higher Self is the main purpose of our life—our main goal is to realize our holy God-created Self. Along the way we do things. We become a lawyer, a doctor, a father, a mother, an artist, an author or what have you. Career is held high on the list of personal attributes that seem to define us. Having a satisfactory career in the vibration of serving others is helpful in Self-realization, yet a good career does not necessarily liberate us from a pervading sense of something missing. It is in this moment of facing the limited character of the personality in which this quest for Self-realization begins. Who am I beyond this mortal, limited, and relative self I made up? In the question is the invocation of a new energy of detachment. Renunciation of lower-level concerns of self-improvement opens new possibilities of Self-realization. The spiritual masters take on new meaning. They are ones who have made direct contact with this Higher Self, and the example of their lives and teachings now becomes the road map we follow. Unconditional Love is fully realized in them. Forgiveness is complete, and they abide in the Absolute holiness of pure being. Through them we are given the boon of Boundless Mercy.

21

We Stand at the Doorway

Liberation is merely rising above our lower nature and negative thoughts and memories that keep us stuck in limitation. There is no limitation in Creation. All things are possible; therefore, we are unlimited spiritual beings stuck in the illusion of littleness we justify to hold ourselves back. Liberation is freedom from the little "self" we made. To step into the expansiveness of our true Self is our greatest inner yearning. We must forgive ourselves for wasting so much of our life stuck, preoccupied with doubt, fear, limitation, and littleness. We stand at the doorway into the Heaven of our true Being and hesitate to go in, as though it is for another place and time, perhaps when we clean up our act, or add one more accolade or feather in our cap, or it is reserved for the future "afterlife." Heaven is a decision we must make *now*. The "doorway" into it is an act of surrender, a complete letting go of the past, and a total forgiveness of everyone and everything, including mostly ourselves. Liberation, Freedom, Forgiveness, Salvation are all the same in this light—in this one decision we must make. Defense and attack have no meaning in the light of this decision. Neither do thoughts of limitation and lack. The Divine Mother of the Cosmos meets all our physical needs. There are no strangers or enemies because we are all One. This shift into the Higher Self is the whole purpose of living. But knowing this is the issue is not enough. Stepping through the doorway to Heaven meets with great resistance. This step is not possible without the benevolent boon of Boundless Mercy.

22

Decide

When you make happiness a decision you must make, rather than a reaction to conditions going on around you, then happiness is possible to have all the time. You decide to be happy regardless of things going out of your favor— mother died, business is down, can't seem to lose weight, house just got flooded. These are external events which have negative thoughts and memories in the mind that reproduced them. The dual nature of thought makes a "hell" in opposition to "heaven." Memory is full of negative, painful experiences. These memories replay in the present. Yet we always have a choice to forgive ourselves for those subconscious thoughts which attract our *hell*—what "we do not want." When we embrace these things "we do not want" as lessons that are showing us the thoughts we need to forgive and let go, then we can appreciate the condition life is showing us. All results, in this way, are steppingstones to total freedom from discontent. I am happy to receive the lessons in my life that are showing me negative aspects of my mind which need to be forgiven and released. In this present moment, the decision for heaven can be made; it is not dependent on external conditions being a certain way. Needs are met in a simple way, and beyond these essential elements, happiness becomes unconditional when you decide that it is so. Decide for heaven now, and don't go back to problems that have been already solved. In this way you invoke the grace of Boundless Mercy.

23

The Miracle of Undoing

Boundless Mercy is an action of life which puts us in heaven now, even though we have made up the problems of hell in our present situations. Miracles undo the causative thought forms, memories, which have attracted the hell. Gratitude is the most practical way to invoke this shift. Forgiveness is an action, too, when we fully understand it. Forgiveness is an "internal job," one in which we become 100 percent responsible for everything which seems to "happen to us." Just as God is the cause for pure joy, separation from God in us is the "cause" of all problems. Thoughts, which are "thought" in this separation produce unhappy effects. Forgiveness is 1) taking 100 percent responsibility for these thoughts, 2) saying I am sorry for these thoughts, 3) allowing these thoughts to be neutralized by Divine Intelligence in order to correct the mind, and 4) being open for the new thoughts we think with God, which bring the manifestations of pure joy. Whoever is willing to do this will bring Boundless Mercy into their awareness. We become free of problems in the frequency of gratitude. Gratitude and grievances cannot occupy our attention simultaneously. Like love and hate cannot operate in the same space; love excludes all hate like hate makes conditions in which love cannot enter. The miracle is a decision to undo all opposition to pure joy, the result of Truth, Simplicity, Love, and Service which is the expression of these eternal principles to others, complete the circle of Boundless Mercy. Heaven is seen. It is always here, but we have been distracted into hell. Only Heaven is real.

24

A Teacher's Role

The role of a teacher who is interested in the souls of the students is to help them evolve and awaken themselves from the dreams of the ego. These are dreams of fear, limitation, doubt, insecurity, etc. A teacher is responsible for undoing beliefs, opinions, judgments in the minds of the students. My teacher, Tara Singh, did this for me. His teacher, Krishnamurti, did that for him. So, this "undoing process" is handed down. It forms a lineage of enlightenment in which eons of time are saved because, with the help of the teacher, the student is liberated from self-deceptions that otherwise would have gone on, unchecked and unexposed. It is not a comfortable process to let go of the ego, usually. In the process of letting go of fear, fear is no longer suppressed. One feels the fear more in the overcoming of fear. Things seems to get "worse" before they get "better." A real life teacher will mentor a student through this process, even though the student may attack him for making his life worse. The mud was always there in the subconscious, yet the internal observation stirs it up and clouds the water in the mind. Only more love will do the job, but the student may run away from the teacher's correction. The ego perceives the correction as an attack and is "hurt" by it. Therefore, the teacher is seen as the "cause of pain," not the liberator who restores the true Self. This is hard for both the teacher and the student. The teacher tries everything to "break through" the resistance of the student, and the student is unwilling to accept the Boundless Mercy of his correction.

25

Relationships

Some relationships have a shelf life. They lose their potency, their original spark which made them attractive in the beginning—with so much promise—and enter into a stagnant phase, even a sad and remorseful place. The early reasons for the relationship have grown up, flowered, withered on the stem, and dropped onto the molding earth. New growths come in. New directions take two people on paths away from each other. We were treating as equal those who are not equal, attempting to raise up the dead from the shadows of limiting thoughts and beliefs. There is a point in which we must let go completely and allow each individual soul to sink or rise on their own, according to their own impetus and inertia. This is a day of reckoning. There is no condemnation in it, but rather a necessity to let all things be exactly as they are. I was given the holy relationships with Sondra Ray, Tara Singh, Muniraj, and through them to the Higher Self of the Divine Mother, Jesus, and Babaji. To pass through these "teachers in a body," to these "teachers in the spirit," is a necessary stage. How one treats these teachers in the body is a test to make contact with these teachers in the spirit. If I betray the trust of the first, how can I merit the latter? I would never know the true teachers of the spirit without a direct relationship with those teachers who are actually in my life, in a body. Therefore, how I treat these actual flesh and blood relationships is paramount. Boundless Mercy surrounds them.

26

A Trusting Expectation

"Trade your nightmares in for happy dreams." Facing our demons without fear and turning over all concerns to the Great Unknown—the Holy Spirit—for the solution best for all, is the beginning of Happy Dreams. We think we need to "fix" things that have gone off. Often the actions we take to fix a relationship or a situation make it worse. At some point we see we do not know what actions to take to restore harmony to a relationship. We can turn it over before we get to this difficult juncture, but we usually don't. The tendency to manage things on our own without the help of the Holy Spirit, pushes us forward into actions that add even more ineffectual attempts to fix things. You cannot fix a nightmare. You are either in it, in which case you believe all the events and characters acting out the miserable drama are real, or you awaken from the dream and feel immediate relief that the whole scenario was just a bad movie in your mind. The happy dream may still elude us, yet a least we know the tragedy is over and we can only go up from here. This action of "turning things over" to a Higher Power must be practical. Rather than a blind faith in which bliss is a pretense, a trusting expectation that things will shift in everyone's favor is the order of the day. A happy dream begins with the accepting of "what is" as the beginning of perfection, even though it may appear to be less than desirable. A dream is still a dream, but a happy dream is the story of Boundless Mercy.

27

Truth is Always Present

Truth is in us whether we are aware of it or not. Truth is Joy. Every time we are not feeling the Joy of Truth, we are not aware of it; we are making something "false" into the "truth." Sadness, pain, grief, depression are feelings that arise when the Truth is not recognized. Truth is always present, yet we are absent. My teacher, Tara Singh, lived in the Presence of Truth. He could even transmit the Joy which accompanies it, and, therefore, all those in the vortex of this Presence felt the Joy as well. They were touched by the Truth through him. The function of a true teacher touches the lives of his students, lifting them to levels of their own being they could not reach on their own without his help. Spiritual masters live by the Truth, by the Absolute, which is free of all opposites. They live by Laws of Love which are whole and undivided, not by lower "laws" of crime and punishment which perpetuate right vs. wrong, innocence vs. guilt, order vs. chaos. They rise above all opposites. Therefore, the Joy they experience and transmit never deviates into sorrow of any kind. They do not oppose the worldly laws of government which maintain a certain order in society, but they insist upon application of the absolute Law of Love which supersedes social order. They live in the spiritual Order of the Timeless, which is the very energy which maintains the cosmos. Their concern is to be consistent with the eternal law of Boundless Mercy.

28

Focused on Fulfillment

We often pretend to be happy when we are just holding back the divulgence of discontent. To keep up appearances in a routine of general maintenance, denial takes a lot of energy. Perhaps just telling the truth, noticing the "contrast" between what you want but have not yet manifested, but aspiring to the new, is better than pretending what you have now is okay. Gratitude for what is now starts a shift because in a state of gratitude you acknowledge 100 percent responsibility. The things you don't like are reflections of your own mind, so they show you the thoughts you need to change. A program of changing your thoughts, a spiritual discipline, is necessary. You can speak in the present what you would like to be so. Even if it has not manifested yet, speaking the positive aspects of your life or what you want to be your life, is far better than complaining or enumerating the articles of your discontent. I tend to be focused on the brutal honesty of what is not working, rather on the vision of the way I want things to be. The only reason one should note the negative is to forgive it and release it faster and faster. Silence is the right transitional response when one feels the discontent. Through the discontent one discovers that the positive aspects are needed to fulfill a desire. When the mind is focused on fulfillment, Boundless Mercy helps you get it.

29

The Waking-Up Process

We live in an age in which everything is provided easily and effortlessly at the push of a button or the click of a mouse. Technological prowess is our forte. And cyber information and social media is at our fingertips. Yet all of this "know how" does not really address the internal questions of meaning and purpose. Each person has a destiny to realize how he or she fits into the greater design of the cosmos but gets distracted by the concerns of physical survival. There has to be the leisure to ponder the reason we are here. The enlightened beings would say we are here to awaken our real Self, which is Love. Yet, we find in this process of waking up, there is a lot in us which is "not Love" in need of undoing. A real teacher focuses on the "not Love" in order to dissolve it through forgiveness. To some this may seem negative in approach, yet how can an obstruction be overcome without recognizing it and removing it? When we take our car to a mechanic to correct a malfunction, he begins immediately to look for the parts not working. The same is true with a spiritual master to whom we go for wisdom. He will begin by pinpointing the thoughts in the mind that are erroneous and "unloving." And through the grace of a person willing to do this deep mental surgery, the mind is cleansed. What a relief that we have masters who give Boundless Mercy.

30

At the Juncture of the Present

What can you say that you have not said before? Each moment of life is unique and different, yet we cover it over with the filter of the past. Is it possible to observe life without this filter? I am sitting at the table in the coffee shop where I have often sat before, writing in this book—like many times already. College students, mostly young females, sit around me working on their Macs; heads buried in their laptops, deeply absorbed in thought. I write by hand with a pen in a blank-paged book, mostly unnoticed by this studious crowd of collegiate. We are always at the juncture of the present, which is presented to us in in raw form with far more observable data than we could possibly absorb. What is the overall thing at hand? Now a multifloored bookstore, systematized in the most efficient way to serve the public, this depository of printed knowledge rivals any library of an ancient age. We used to go to lending libraries for our books. Now we go to Amazon online or to a Barnes & Noble superstore. Yet the same observances apply—what is really new and original? Amidst more facility to acquire a book and more opportunity to have a coffee while reading the most enticing periodical, we still sit in relative isolation from one another. The notion of a "stranger" is still a major obstacle to spiritual connection to wholeness. Love, being everywhere, in all things, simultaneously forever, evades our awareness. We are held hostage by this sense of separation, only to be freed by Boundless Mercy.

31

We Remain Tribal

Superficiality stays focused on the surface level of life, with the aspects of appearance and the sentimentality of personal preferences in the forefront of presentation. Profiles define us as what we do, what we know, who we know, what food we eat, what friends we post pictures of on Facebook, and an endless variety of aspects which limit us to a collection of self-made qualities. The spiritual depth is always present, yet who is looking toward a broader, deeper reality of life? We have replaced churches with yoga centers and meet-up groups. A set of exercises and a bunch of people liking the same thing are the new dogmas which attract the collective consciousness. We remain tribal, identified by the Facebook groups we belong to. Sex and money, the two biggest concerns of daily life, still dominate consciousness as we formulate our activities around them. They are the hooks which marketers target, the areas of the most "pain" which motivate people to act, to pursue with the investment of their energy, attention, and life. What is the real purpose of existence? A vision of holiness is very seldom listed in a university curriculum. It is not in the Help Wanted ads. You will not see employers requiring "sainthood" as a quality needed to get the job. Yet the purpose of life is to realize your universal, unlimited Self. All the social cards are mute. They need infusion of Boundless Mercy.

32

Claiming our True Inheritance

Happiness is a recognition of truth. Truth is inherently happy. The nature of the cosmos is Joy. This Joy is absolute; therefore, having no opposite. Physical forms manifest then go back to the unmanifest. All is innocent in this process of taking a form and returning to the formless. What is ever-present is Joy. In the arena of human affairs, an opposite arises—sorrow—to usurp the sovereignty of Joy. It is a choice we make and with all choices, it seems two options are possible. There is a "branching in the road" and we have a chance to go one way or the other. Only one will satisfy our desire to live in harmony with the Divine Forces of Life. One is leading toward truth, toward Joy, toward a universal connection to the whole, and the other is fraught with problems, conflicts, disappointments, divisions, factions, and the like. Only happiness is true. What is not happy is made up—a false scenario we project onto the Life Force. Life leads us to more Joy. The belief in death causes a deep sense of grief, even sorrow. This is because we "identify" so heavily with the body, and we believe it will age and die. Then we get what we believe, and this makes us sad. The freedom from belief leads us away from sorrow. Even the body can be put under the domain of the Spirit, and thus transcend even death. The truth of a joyous life is always our true inheritance, yet we must claim it to be so. In this decision abides the strength of Boundless Mercy.

33

The Limitless I AM

I AM. There is a power of Being which is expressed with I AM. God said to Moses, "I AM that I AM." He did not put anything after I AM because that would have been a "limitation." "God is in everything I see" is lesson #29 in A Course in Miracles. Everything is everything which is a whole cosmos. God extends into infinity, even beyond shape and form, even beyond the Word, the Idea of everything. ACIM goes on to say, "God is in my mind." This mind is also God's mind. They are unified by this lesson, by this Truth. We go along in life maintaining our memories, our possessions, our relationships with people, our jobs, our belief systems—which all keep us very limited when it comes to realizing our greatest Self. I am this or that. I am a carpenter who builds homes with wood. It takes good craft to please my customers. This good craft does not rely on having the best tools alone—it relies on a commitment to accuracy, precision, completion in a thorough way, and in a timely fashion. This good craft helps the carpenter be a good success and have his own house, family, sense of purpose. Yet even this is not the full expression of his Being, "I AM." I am as God created me, who is limitless like God. This is an open declaration of liberation from all lower levels of Being. "I am the holy Son of God Himself," Lesson #191. Who is willing to claim this Self-identity and be free? It is the Truth, yet can we live by the truth? It is the full expression of happiness and Joy. It is the invocation of Boundless Mercy.

34

Bed, Bath & Beyond

The first thing we do in the morning sets the stage for the rest of the day, therefore an orderly and joyful start is essential. We make the bed together. This action may seem mundane or insignificant, but it is one of the most important actions that determine all the rest in how your day will unfold. If you don't make the bed, and leave behind unfinished and disheveled sheets and covers, then this disorder permeates the next thing you do in your day. So, make your bed! It will make you feel good, especially if you make it together with your mate. The next thing to do is take a shower. Bathing in the morning is water purification. You can also light a candle or a small fire for fire purification. We honor the elements and express gratitude for our physical existence by doing so. After showering and getting dressed, which includes all the normal hygiene of brushing your teeth and combing your hair, it is good to sit down and meditate on something transcendental. We have particular things we attend to in our meditations, such as Sanskrit mantras, writings of gratitude, A Course in Miracles, etc. But all you really need to do is sit and observe your thoughts in a semi-detached way. Eventually you will identify less with the thoughts you think and more with the empty space between these thoughts. This brings in a great stillness and silence, which put Peace in the forefront of your life. Don't you want this good start to your day? Bed, Bath & Beyond. These are the three first actions of any day that give you Boundless Mercy.

35

Thankfulness

Thanksgiving for family is important throughout the year, not just on one designated day in which a feast is customary. The peace of God covers the family on every day. I call it in to envelope my parents, my sister, my wife, and all related to us. Should a crisis arise, I trust that God will give us the solution. I give thanks for my inner connection to the Divine—times I spend listening for any communication that comes from the Greater Whole. "God's voice speaks to me all through the day," is lesson #49 in A Course in Miracles. The problem is often I am not paying attention, not listening in a manner that can hear what He is saying. Today I am listening to God's voice and what He has to say about Thanksgiving. All thanks are to God, of God, and for God. The thanks we give to everything else is included in this divine acknowledgement, because "everything else" is God as well. God is in our family members, equally, although each member may not be aware of this fact equally. A holy person is just someone who pays attention to God more frequently than others do. He is immersed in the Thanksgiving for Life to his Creator. He is also immersed in the everyday affairs that concern us all, with the intention to bring divine awareness into those affairs. People, and even whole nations, can feel "wronged" by others. This makes up a notion of vengeance, the exact opposite of Thanksgiving. In a crisis in which it is easy to feel "wronged," it is important to remain thankful. This attitude of gratitude is what will move us through the crisis and keep us in the graces of Boundless Mercy.

36

Blessed Bali

Bali, the "island of the Gods," has a holy energy that one can feel. Beauty abounds and houses become temples which integrate art, architecture, and nature. The people are in a constant worship of Life. We saunter the streets of Ubud observing the unique energy of the shops and restaurants. There are a few things that we buy—mala beads of jade and tiger's eye, a colorful carving, some batik clothing, etc. Yet the real encounter with the mercy of the Divine Mother comes at the Besakih Temple a couple hour's drive away from our villas, an exceptional place of holy ascension. Our friends were with us on this pilgrimage to the top of the seventh level, where the element of space is most apparent. All concerns drop away as the mind comes to stillness and quiet. A patch of bamboo forms the alter. The presence of nothing is in stark contrast to the elaborate temple structures built on the lower levels. As one ascends, the man-made becomes less and less, and the God-created becomes more and more. There is an etheric presence at the top of the Besakih Temple, a place where divine beings congregate. They meet up here to participate in the holy Joy of real existence and to invite those beings who are ready to participate in Heaven on Earth. All the blessings of this trip to Bali have lined up perfectly. We are among the gods who draw us here to experience the divine heights of human existence. They continue to bestow on us Boundless Mercy.

37

Journeys Far and Near

The travel that we embark upon is to truly make our individual will consistent with the Universal Will. This is the purpose of real yoga when God's vibration and our vibration are One. Jesus said, "I and my Father are One." He was a fully realized yogi, and his words were consistent with God's words. This is a lesson we need to get, and we must live by the truth of words that are of God; therefore, the expressions of God's will. All travel is a journey to our own awakening in this Union. The journey could take us halfway around the world to Bali or India, or it could take us to the depths of our real mind while sitting in a chair at home. It is not about a place or a proximity, although a journey to a sacred site which has been established in its true holiness can aid us in this union with Divine Will. A holy place exudes a holy vibration; in its presence our vibration is lifted more easily. This is the whole purpose of a true pilgrimage to a holy site. If the site is pure and true it will lift you up by virtue of its holiness. This could also happen in your kitchen if you have dedicated it rightly to God's will of feeding God's children. When you feed another from the Joy of divine sustenance, that establishes that place as a holy site. Your own home can be this when properly dedicated. A being who has truly joined his will with the universal will of God lives in a holy home. The holy home is anywhere that being abides because he is in a constant contact with Boundless Mercy.

38

Connection

A human being consciously connected to his or her Divine Source sees other human beings connected to theirs, even if they are not aware of this connection. Whatever lives would not be alive without this Divine Source of connection. A unified field of Life is unified in every atom, molecule, entity, and celestial body. All is connected; that is what makes it a unified field. Every human being in this unified field of the Cosmos is connected and therefore joined with every other human being. Each human being is also connected to the trees, the mountains, the sky, the rivers, the animals, and the stars as well. In fact, he or she is connected to everything in the Cosmos. Connection implies shared identity. Identity implies a Self. This Self I am is connected to every atom, molecule, entity, body or all the elements in the Cosmos—therefore this Self I am is connected to everything. This being so in the unified field, it is also true that every human being is connected to every other human being, as a shared Self. It would follow that any action taken toward another is an action I take toward myself. To harm another is to harm myself. To offer healing to another is to offer it to myself. This confirms the statement, "To give and to receive are one in truth." Whatever I give my brother, who is my Self, I receive as well. Therefore, I give Boundless Mercy.

39

The Spiritual Traveler Observes

A journey taken to the other side of the planet transforms a person, even if they are not so aware of the transformation. Open to a new vision, a spiritual traveler would be attentive to the differences—and similarities—a foreign culture would have to his own. The differences are always beneficial because they expand his horizons one way or the other. A country not so developed, with over population, may invoke a sense of gratitude for all one has back home. Yet even amidst the negative shortcomings of these underprivileged situations, the foreign land may have assets of the heart which far exceed the development in the West. People care for one another in ways that exceed material prowess and possession. They exhibit an inner joy which is not affected by external conditions. This propensity for happiness rises above all striving for improvement. A certainty pervades the very being of people so connected to their Divine Source that every movement acknowledges and strengthens this connection. In Bali, people live as gods. Every day is an unfolding of devotion. Every minute is spent in the service of pure joy. These are the observances of a Westerner who is looking for holiness of a land, rather than dwelling on the negative shortcomings. Not all live in the essence of their own land. Plenty of Americans live in bondage to many things—jobs, debt, illness, appetites—amidst a vibration that is free and liberated at the very core. Living as gods is the essence of Bali, yet not all choose to live in this essence. Those who do possess Boundless Mercy.

40

No Sacrifice Necessary

Let me flee to the thing I really want and give up nothing as I hasten to God realization. "I am not asked to make a sacrifice to find the mercy and the peace of God." The conditions for finding this peace are easy because there are no conditions. Nothing must be pre-arranged or "accomplished" to awaken into the truth of who we are as God created us. Many have thought they must "give up" what they want in order to receive something that they "want" more. The truth of Self-identity does not require any giving up of anything real. The pleasure-pain dichotomy of physical existence dissolves in the Joy of God. Could any call this a sacrifice? "I can give up but what was never real" and "I gladly make the 'sacrifice' of fear." (ACIM Lessons 322-323) These thoughts are clearly "giving up" nothing, so the notion of sacrifice is totally undone in the truth of these statements of Jesus in A Course in Miracles. In the Joy of God, realized in this lifetime, we still experience "a body." But now the body is in the service of the mind, and the mind is in the service of forgiveness. And both mind and body are in service to Truth—I am spirit. Spirit is neither mind nor body, although it imbues both with the Joy of God. Who can say Love is a body? The whole Cosmos is engulfed by it. Love defies definition, yet no one denies its Presence as the Essence behind the best and brightest Light of Life. To be in the awareness of Love is to be God-realized. The age which thought sacrifice was necessary for this realization is over. We are now in the age of Boundless Mercy.

41

At Day's End

The night comes upon us and our activities of the day come to an end. For those free of television and its innumerable distractions, there is space to read and write, spend time with a spouse or a family member, or just sit quietly and observe one's thoughts. The quiet of the night profoundly envelops everything around me. The loudest sound is the hum of the refrigerator motor, or the drone of the furnace that blows its winter heat through the numerous ducts that are in each room of the apartment. I can hear the smooth scratching of the pen across this paper as I write. What is there to say when all daily tasks have been laid aside? In a pause there is stillness and silence. These are the gifts of introspection which come about when attention is given to the Life in the present. There is nothing artificial in these observances. A Peace comes over my awareness by virtue of giving attention to the present, without the usual distraction. No TV. No iPhone. No computer. No telephone. No duties to perform. No additional interests other than coming to the Peace and Joy of a quietude. How reluctant one would become to return to the world of work, of toil, of external concerns. Yet this return is to a place that does not exist in reality as long it governs itself with the notions of death. Is it more likely you could pay homage to the Mother of the universe and have a real appreciation for the new awareness of exactly "what is." This is exactly what comes to you as well. It comes in Boundless Mercy.

42

The One Need

Fondly, and with great expectation, one approaches the possibility—and necessity—of miracles. For without a positive faith, anticipation of a likely shift in the situation at hand, which does all but deny a shift, miracles would not be possible. We come to them in some sort of need, usually, to set right something that has gone—sometimes terribly—wrong. We call for a miracle in a time of tribulation when we have exhausted the attempts of our own to escape from trouble. As the trouble persists in spite of our attempts to resolve it, the helplessness we face at the very end of our string of ineffective "solutions" becomes the very invocation for supernatural Forces, which are inherently benevolent to our necessity—to step in to resolve things in our sincere time of need. The need could be seen as various, endlessly changing to an equally varied set of circumstances. Yet, the real need is most always ONE. The one need is connection to our Source, to full awareness of who we are as God created us. We do not have a multitudinous array of needs. This ONE need looms in every pursuit to fulfill our happiness. All liberty is in it because it is the only real freedom we seek from the travails of daily living. Above the level of mere survival, the connection to God places us in the domain of Heaven on Earth that dissolves all other concerns. This is the real Source of Creativity and all things bright and beautiful. This connection is the realm of Boundless Mercy.

43

Correction and Connection

The inner work of self-correction is a passion, or it is not. Until we do this work, we remain in various degrees separated from our divine function. There are ideas and negative thoughts—illusions, in essence, which we nevertheless believe in the core of our being. Until these are cleared completely through a most rigorous process of self-inquiry and radical forgiveness, we hold ourselves back from expressing and extending our true Self. Certain conditions in life are helpful to this Self-awakening: 1) that we are aware that we do not know our Self as we could, 2) that we are determined to know It, and 3) we are willing to accept the help of a master who does know his/her true Self. These three conditions are necessary for Self-awakening. Without having a master, these points would not be so clear. Having been with Tara Singh for 17 years gave me the love of inner correction. This work requires attention at levels that must be awakened. The first thing a master will point out is that what you "know" is the root of the problem. We think "knowledge" liberates us from a low life, yet it can bind us to beliefs and conflicts that keep us blind to our Absolute Self. Memory, beliefs, the very content of our minds that we call knowledge has not liberated man from suffering and sorrow. Divided and separated, the human thought system of relative knowledge keeps one from connection to the Source, to God, to the true Self. A real master transcends relative knowledge to make contact with the absolute of Boundless Mercy.

44

No Greater Joy

The Joy of knowing who we are as God created us is unsurpassed. No greater Joy exists. This is the primary relationship that imbues all other relationships with a similar Joy. The mystics and the poets know this; the composers and the artists know this; the great men of science know this; the saints and the women who embrace true motherhood know this: only God is true, and only Love is true. God, Love, and Joy are all One. And every human being is created in this vibration originally. The person who knows the Self is inherently connected to all his brothers and sisters; to love God and to love his fellow human beings is the same. Separation has ended for him or her. Life becomes a song, a painting of intense beauty, a story of remarkable characters who compose a drama of divine proportions. Five seconds of this vision is worth one's whole life. Ascension into these realms of Truth lifts one out of all problems. This vision is who you are as God created you. This vision is unforgettable and renders all other sight obsolete. In the presence of One who lives in this vision, a person is taken into the vortex of their influence, making the ascension not only possible but truly inevitable. When a person yearns to know the Truth above all else in life, the true teacher is provided. Compassion from the teacher to the student is so vast, it verges on the Cosmic. It is of Boundless Mercy.

45

A Vision of Wholeness

God consciousness and Pure Joy are the same. What does a person need to be conscious of in order to know God (which would automatically lend to Pure Joy)? We have the five senses: touch, smell, taste, hearing, and visual sight. We have the sixth sense of the mind, of insight, of awareness. Applied to the other five senses, awareness transcends the mere sensations of physical objects in order to form relationships that lead to a vision of wholeness, oneness, unification. God-consciousness and this vision of wholeness are the same. The lesson, "To Love my Father is to Love His Son," makes it very clear that Love of God, or God-consciousness, is connected to Love of our fellow human beings. (ACIM Lesson #246) And since God created every human being on the planet, to "Love His Son" is to Love everybody. This does not mean everyone's behavior is "Love-worthy," but everyone's behavior is certainly "forgiveness-worthy." So, the doorway to loving everyone is through forgiveness. We must distinguish between the behavior and the essence of the person, whether he or she is acting from that essence or not. A misdirected soul may kill another, thinking that soul is dead, but the soul lives on and cannot be killed. In essence the murderer has done nothing but attack Love, attack immortality, which cannot really be threatened. When a person has a vision of even forgiving murder, he or she is much closer to this "vision of wholeness." Pure Joy cannot turn to sorrow. It is Absolute, without opposite. It is Boundless Mercy.

46

The Place of Happiness

The place of happiness is inside of us. But usually we are associating external conditions with our happiness; if these conditions align with what we want, all is okay. But if plans run contrary to our wishes, our happiness is threatened. What if the external conditions had nothing to do with real happiness? The source of our happiness is the same as our Source of Life. Our Source created us, and the nature of this Source is happiness, free of all conditions. Our connection to this Source Energy is what can bring into us a happiness that is unaffected by the externals. Beauty is perceived as a relationship of Divine order and harmony that makes us feel uplifted. But the sense of order and harmony is already in us, so we can see this harmony in aspects of the external that align with it. A view of nature can impart to us this sense of beauty. A piece of art, a painting, or a sculpture can transmit these relationships of harmony that are already in us. But in the situations that are discordant there is a need to make contact with the internal happiness that is the Source of all things. A universal Joy is always accessible to our consciousness, yet we must invoke this connection until it becomes so prevalent that we are in it all the time. Most of us depend on external conditions being just right in order to be happy. Some people are never happy. But God's will for us is perfect happiness; therefore, to be happy is an act of will. This will is Boundless Mercy.

47

Real Freedom

We live in a universe of abundance. As human beings inhabiting the earth, we often forget that universal forces are on our side. The old paradigm of "man against nature" coupled with the hunter mindset made for a world of tribal and territorial rites. They divided humans into separate groups and societies and introduced the concept of ownership, "me and mine," which in turn invited competition into the picture. With this came fear. Will I prevail over the forces that seem indifferent, or even hostile, to my needs, or will I be swept away by these forces? Survival entered the mind of humankind, with all of its struggles and travails. Men, identifying with the animals of nature, fell into this survival of the fittest rule of the land. Kings at the top of this "food chain" took the lion as their mascot and symbol—an animal which had no other predator above it. Power through dominance and ability to kill became the false prerequisites for safety. The use of fear over others became the tactic for governance and domination. Then came an experiment in the new world: In God we trust, one nation under God, with liberty and justice for all. Freedom from fear, freedom from a sense of lack, and freedom from another's domination is the only real freedom. In this awareness the self of fear is replaced by the Self of Love, Peace, and Joy. This is a freedom of Boundless Mercy.

48

The Source is In Us

A common experience we all have is family, growth, relating to the elements of Life. Yet where, when, and how we incarnate has vast variations of culture, education, economic facility, personal talents and interests. Within this field of influence there seems an endless set of choices, actions, and motives to be considered in one's life. Do we turn our God-given talents and the skills we have perfected over to the survival level of existence, or give them over to discovering the Source and Glory of why we took birth in the first place? Much of what we do has an end result in mind. What is the result we labor and struggle to maintain? We all say we want more Peace, Joy, and happiness, but do these states of being exist in the "more or less"? They are Absolute states that have no incremental degrees. One is either in a state of Pure Joy, or one is not. What we call Joy is often temporary gratification which comes and goes. I was happy about the events of yesterday, but today I am sad. This sort of happiness that can be replaced by its opposite is not Pure Joy. The Source of Pure Joy is not here today and gone tomorrow. So, what is the "object of joy" is not the Source of Joy. The Source is not its form of expression of experience. Our connection with this Source of Life is fundamental when we are not distracted by seeking it or trying to attain it externally. The Source is in us. Giving attention to this Source is the basis of meditation. When all seeking ceases, our true Source emerges as Boundless Mercy.

49

You are a Rose

Praise is a high vibration, especially when it is of the Cosmic Forces which created us. I wrote a whole book of praise to the Divine Mother. These writings were done over a period of four years, much in the same way I am writing these pages on Boundless Mercy. These are one-page meditations, written in long hand, in an Italian leather-bound journal. In this highly busy world in which attention deficit seems to be the order of the day, one page is about all anyone can handle. We are moving too fast from one sound bite to the other to devote any more than a few minutes to reading or listening at any one time. If the thing does not grip us immediately and temporarily shake us out of our current momentum, we move on to the next stimulus without much digestion of the morsel we have consumed. My way of addressing this status quo of flitting from one thing to the next without stopping to smell the roses, is to give praise to a "rose" on one page that is so aromatic that the aftermath of its fragrance lingers on in the nasal chambers of our fast-moving senses. Slow down! These twenty minutes of writing can be read in two minutes, yet the praise of the rose is a timeless and universal encounter embedded in the psyche of nearly every human being. Who does not feel uplifted by blooms for a day? I am engulfed in praise. The fragrance of these few moments I spend with You, my reader, are the roses which form the bouquet of beautiful arrangement. You are my rose, and this one page of sharing a flower of Boundless Mercy.

50

Gratitude for Conveniences

Winter brings the cool air and the snow. In the United States of America, we are fortunate to have the modern conveniences of central heating in our homes, so we are not so affected by the climate. Indoors and cozy, we are grateful to be free of chopping wood, filling the coal bin, or keeping the fire lit during this cold season. We just set the thermostat and forget it, and when we feel a little chilly, turn it up a few degrees. What could be easier? Of course, then we pay the electric bill at the end of the month, which is generally higher in the winter. There are other conveniences which we take for granted, but just 100 years ago were not so prevalent. My mother spoke of having an "outhouse," which was a toilet outside, apart from the main house. Now we have centralized plumbing with water flowing at the turn of a handle and toilets that flush with water-saving efficiency. The winter is a good time to stay indoors and appreciate the beauty of these modern wonders. People thought a lot about these inventions, and they have become perfected over the years. We must not forget much of the human population does not have them, but for whatever good karma, we do. We in the USA are the recipients of Boundless Mercy. The resources we have in this land, coupled with the "can do" spirit, makes everything possible. To use those resources wisely, not to waste, to have a constant contact with gratitude is to be surrounded by Boundless Mercy.

51

Meeting the Wise

Connection with another, verging even on communion, is a sharing so deep that the separation between two people ceases. What are the conditions for this kind of sharing? One must be free of ulterior motives. If I want to get something from you in our encounter, then the connection only exists to the degree you fill my needs. If I want to give you something that would in turn render you in my debt, that is also motive ridden. A motiveless sharing is rare. One approaches it with no needs and no expectations. Sharing on this level springs from inspiration that has its own action. We are inspired by the words of the wise in our desire to live by them and make them our own truth. Our relationship with the wise is a "communion" of sorts, yet we are still approaching it as getting something we may not yet have: ("I hear the truth, but I see I am not living it. Therefore, I endeavor to apply it to my life.") We cannot yet meet the wise on equal ground until we have applied a truth. Yet the wise sense that we fall short. There is a "descent" on their part in order to communicate to us, helping us in our "ascent." Somewhere we meet. We meet the wise in the place of absolution. The wise see, but overlook our errors; we see, yet sense we are only aspiring to their truth—their wisdom. This holy relationship is a giving and receiving. It is the basis for real transformation and real communion. The wise give to the universe to make its people wise. This is Boundless Mercy.

52

Communion and Real Connection

In the public domain we notice that communion and real connection are not the status quo: most people are operating at the survival level of acquiring their basic needs—money, food, house, car. Some are engaged in careers that uplift and inspire, yet most find a mechanical function in a system that fulfills certain human needs, and for this they are rewarded accordingly. This mechanical function can deny the human being a higher function of communion. But not always. The poet Kabir, who made contact with very real transcendental states, also worked as a weaver of cloth. Having made contact with his own Divine nature, all actions after that became imbued with this vibration of unlimited glory—even in the weaving of cloth. A seeming separation of levels—the Divine Spirit versus the "hard stuff" of a material world—is dissolved by the one-pointed attention of a saint who has embraced both as equally holy. This embrace transcends the level of survival. Yet, the public domain is not the catalyst for this transcendence, though it could be the matrix that holds a place for it to happen. We are all in this public domain to some degree, so we "know it." What we may not know is some Divine Connection that needs some other factor, outside the public domain of influence. Divine Connection arises in a person's awareness when he or she meets another whose Divine Connection is strong. This person may be in the public domain, weaving cloth. But the real connection springs forth from Boundless Mercy.

53

Overcome Isolation

People are isolated by many things: circumstances, personality traits, economic status, levels of education, national and language barriers, etc. Yet, they are connected to the wholeness of life in reality. Everyone on the planet breathes the same air, drinks the same water, sees the light of day come over the horizon, and is blanketed by dark the rest of the night. We come into an awareness of this greater connection when we practice gratitude for this life and ask the question of the purpose for our presence here on Earth. When the cosmic order of things is given attention, an even larger field of existence comes into play. Preponderance of the non-physical realm takes us to a place in the mind even more vast. Millions of galaxies that each contain millions of stars and solar systems are big enough, yet, the Great Void of Nothing— out of which everything sprang forth—is even beyond our comprehension in scope. What could there be beyond that? Even light is contained by this level vaster than the infinite. The human being within the Great Void proceeds into Cosmic Being in Creation and therefore is imbued into every possible molecule of universal magnificence. A vision of this deep connection takes shape through a relationship with another human being who has his or her eyes opened to real sight already. This holy relationship opens our eyes to the truth as well. A true teacher gives the strength to overcome isolation and join with the wholeness of Boundless Mercy.

54

In the Wake of Current Change

There is change in the realm of human relationships not always in the way we expect or desire. These are shifts that can reform the field of play or alter the course of action altogether. A one hundred eighty-degree turnaround can be shocking, yet even this can be for the better. New results are about to unfold from the Unknown, yet one is clear the scene is "out of control." This is a good thing. Control is often limited by our plans and expectations. To give this up is to be free; yet fear of the Unknown can come up. What result is worth the upset of fear? Even if it is Unknown, why would you expect something bad to happen? Trust is more all-pervasive than expectations and control. Trust is a certainty that all movements and changes are for the good. New situations come out of the old, and growth is better than stagnation. There is a level of reality which cannot be threatened by change. In this world change is often feared because the status quo has become comfortable and known; to change the status quo could introduce the Unknown. No longer familiar with the old circumstances, fear of new circumstances arises. This is when trust is needed the most—in the wake of current change. I trust that this change is for the better. I trust that conditions which may have seemed good were flawed, therefore a change was necessary for the correction to take place. Life provides these opportunities for change in which errors are corrected and conditions are made more favorable by virtue of Boundless Mercy.

55

One Goal Only

When we think all is lost, all is found. We are not seeking success, nor relying on our plans to reach our goals. In fact, we have one goal only, and that is to live by Divine Will and be connected to our Source in all we think, say, or do. To the extent we are attached to a plan other than God's plan, when things go awry, we are upset. A peaceful acceptance comes about when we do not attach ourselves to our plan, but rather accept things as they are. Joy is possible in the long term when it is not dependent on a particular outcome. The inner work to do is the detachment from the way things turn out. In this detachment, the opposites of "success" or "failure" have little meaning. Reality is not dualistic; in other words, it does not vacillate between opposites. There is no "opposition" at all in Reality. The orbit of the planets and the laws of nature remain unaffected by human plans. The man or woman who is connected and tapped into this Life Force does not worry about making the right "plans." He has trust that even in the face of the Unknown, Life is moving him along in a direction consistent with God's Love and Cosmic Joy. He brings his own mind to stillness and does not project a "plan" which could fail to be achieved. The order of the universe is always a fact. Are we with it or not? Enlightenment is merely our awareness that does not deviate from this order. In this awareness of order is the boon of Boundless Mercy.

56

A Language of the Heart

In the spaciousness of a Spanish café there is a vista overlooking an urban lake. There I have a coffee with my friend, Lazaro. He speaks no English, nor I Spanish, so we try to say a few words to each other without much understanding. But there is a language of the heart which transcends words. In this communication no words are needed. We are here to relax. I pull out my journal, and he opens his iPad as we sip our coffee and enjoy the cool sea air. In Santa Cruz, Tenerife, there is a relaxed atmosphere. It is a city, yet not as bustling as Madrid or Barcelona. An island off the west coast of Africa, Tenerife is in a group of islands called the Canaries. We sit near the sea observing the sun peeking through a hole in the clouds. For the most part, the days have been gray, and the clouds roll across the sky in an atmosphere of billowing overcast with little opportunity for rays of the sun to shoot forth. But today, there are a few moments of bright warmth spreading through the gray cotton cover. My friend is busy on his iPad, and I am handwriting in my book. It is wonderful to be together with him without the need of words. Hearts join in a camaraderie that do not need speech. We share a silence between us. We share a leisure which does not require any explanation. Human beings naturally commune with one another on a level free of thought. In this space of silence, all the universe is connected. Together in this quiet is the reality of Boundless Mercy.

57

A Blessing to Everyone

The sages of great wisdom are more present than others. They understand the pitfalls and distractions in life that cause suffering, and they are free of these deceptions, so they emanate a stillness and silence that blesses all people, places, and things. Everything is holy in their eyes, and therefore connected in an interrelated Cosmic field of creation. They do not oppose or strive. They flow according to the One Law. The One Law is to be consistent with their very nature, their higher Self. They enter into a realm of glory which does not consist of opposites. In this awareness, Darkness and Light come together to form One Thing. This One Thing envelopes everything in its blanket of holiness, surrounding every atom and molecule with the Love of total acceptance, total Peace and Joy. This One Thing has One Law—it extends its presence to increase the joy of everything else. This sage who has integrated opposites into the One Thing, has done so first within himself. He lives in a forgiven Self which has no conflict. All his past is over and released; his memory is not replaying the battles—won or lost—from his history of traumas and struggles. He does not strive nor plan to achieve because everything already is in a state of perfection. This perfection of the One Thing, operating from the One Law of giving Love, lives to be itself fully right now. It need not become "more perfect" in the future. This wise person is a blessing to everyone he or she meets. Divinely distracted, there is no calling to a future time or place more desirable. Here and now contains the necessary ingredients for Boundless Mercy.

58

The Home that Has No Border

People need a sense of home. Most associate a home with family, residence, state and city, nationality, or some particular ideology. Basically, a tribal mentality forms the notion of a home. "I am a graduate of Harvard." That is a tribe. "I am a Catholic." Another tribe. "I am Chinese." This is a bigger tribe. "I am on Facebook," yet another tribe of influence and conditions. "I am in the Bush family." These all can give a person a sense of belonging, but they are limited to a border, a circumventing fence around the tribe which, when crossed over, places that person in a "homeless" state of being. When a sense of home is lost, there is insecurity and fear. One has no ground to call his "home." What is the real "home" that has no border, no line of demarcation that artificially makes an insider or an outsider? It is interesting that within the word *home* is OM. OM is a Sanskrit word that indicates a vibration which permeates all the Cosmos. Everything in creation vibrates by virtue of a Life Force, and this force is uttered by the sound OM. It contains all things; therefore, it has no end, no edge, no border. It cannot ever be a place one leaves. It has no "outside." It is the one home everyone seeks to find and inhabit. It is a containment of everyone and everything, whether anyone is aware of it or not. We walk around homeless in an ocean of Cosmic peace and joy that is home to everything. When we are aware of this one and real Home, we have entered the domain of Boundless Mercy.

59

The Only Place to Be

"I don't want to be here" is a deep thought embedded in the human psyche. We are of the few species that commit conscious suicide and kill each other. We seek a home of perfect conditions which we seldom find, so we can complain and reinforce our strife and struggle to achieve these elusive, and often imaginary, conditions. Then at some point, disillusionment sets in and we begin to sense the futility of our travail. In this moment, the thought "I don't want to be here" is strong. There may be irreversible conditions—illness, financial loss, death in the family, natural disasters—which contribute to a miserable situation in our life. We then want to be here even less. How do we free ourselves from this thought, "I don't want to be here"? It is at the root of many troubles. It can be the cause of relationships that fail. It can put a business into bankruptcy. How do we embrace our life fully and weather the storm of things gone awry? How do we fully want to be here independent of the shifts and changes of external circumstances? I am as God created me. Peace and Joy are the attributes of this creation. What is not connected to Peace and Joy is not who I am. To stay in the Self-identity of who I am as God created me is to have constant contact with Peace and Joy. This is the only "place" to be—in the awareness of my Self-identity. With increased awareness of Peace and Joy, the desire to be here increases as well. There is no effort in this awareness, so I am responsible to be aware of Self-identity and be Pure Joy. All else is false. Self-identity has Boundless Mercy.

60

Our Natural Inheritance

I seek what already belongs to me—God's Peace and Joy. When all other seeking ends, this is the One Thing God has provided in truth. Truth would undo all the other distractions which do not lead to Peace and Joy. The journey has no distance. Peace and Joy are always in this present moment, yet we are absent. Why do we reject Peace and Joy? Why do we project problems into the life stream which does not have problems? There is the one problem of separation. We have disconnected from the awareness of our Source, and never really tapped into it again. It is not that we are really disconnected from our Source; this is impossible. The life force is giving us life constantly, yet we have lost touch with the gratitude for life itself. We get distracted into a discontent that is so deep we seem to have forgotten that Peace and Joy are our natural inheritance. We make up conditions which determine whether we will be happy or not. When we don't achieve those conditions, we seem to be disconnected from our Source again, which is emanating Peace and Joy. God's attributes are ours to claim without meeting certain conditions. God is a Force so all-encompassing that we scarcely have ever made contact with such a magnitude of Source Energy. If we had made contact with It, all problems would be solved, and we would have awareness of total Peace and Joy. We have forgotten God in our deep sleep. Awakening to reality of our Source seems like a *task*, but no task can awaken. We are awake by virtue of Boundless Mercy.

61

This Tiny Corner of the Cosmos

Into Istanbul, a late arrival in the dark, not quite knowing what to expect. A visa at the airport not so hard. A short glitch put us at the baggage claim late. Some confusion with the visa machine. A man at the window helped us. Free sailing through customs to the exit, where a driver found us coming out. I felt a sigh of relief. Soon we were in his car going into the city. He drove fast on the six-lane highway. I watched the buildings and the red neon letters in a foreign tongue whizz by. Around thirty minutes later we were at an apartment door in a section of town near high-end hotels. A good place. A dark-haired lady greeted us and the driver. We took the elevator up to the fifth floor. It took a few trips to bring up our luggage, as the elevator was small—barely enough room for two people and one case. Soon we were situated in our room. Spacious and clean, we are grateful to be provided for in this new city on the sea, between the East and the West, a bridge of cultures going back centuries. What is in store for us? Who will we meet and teach? It is in God's hands now as we have come with open hearts and minds to receive and give according to higher laws. We are in service of the Divine to the people of Turkey. To Love God is to love them. All one we are on this planet Earth that we inhabit in this tiny corner of the Cosmos. What better place than this. Constantinople could be the scene where we make our bridge to Your Boundless Mercy.

62

Early Morning Listening

It is the morning hour. Sounds of the city echo from below and the heavy machinery sends abrupt sounds of disturbance into the atmosphere. Amidst this cacophony, a dove contributes her melodious refrain and a crow cackles in to complete the urban cantata. A car passes directly below. A door of an automobile closes, and I hear the driver set the alarm with a high-pitched trill. Across the river valley a suspension bridge spans the bay, connecting the two sides of the city. A horn blasts below and I observe a man on the construction site far away in a day-glow yellow jacket. Another man in black sweeps the sidewalk with a broom as three other men hover together smoking cigarettes. By and by they disband, and the tan and white cat scurries across the driveway then stops to assess the terrain. The man sweeping continues to push the debris into a pile. On the horizon far away, some clouds gather in a row and catch the peach color of the sun's illumination just under the thick blanket of gray overcast. My wife riffles through her bag, searching for who knows what, not to be found. She finds her small book in another bag, unexpected. A motorcycle revs up in the symphony of urban sound and speeds off eventually into the far corner of the city. I can be quiet in this early morning listening. For this I am grateful to have the space to observe life as it is. Istanbul is similar to any other city. The constant rumble of movements and motives rise from the earth as I sit in my stillness enjoying the leisure of Boundless Mercy.

63

A Nocturnal Meditation

Now it is night in Istanbul where I find myself in the center of town across from Taksim Square in the warm room provided by our hostess, Dina. It has been a good day. People came to hear us talk tonight on the nature of our work. Liberation Breathing and Loving Relationships were the subjects of our lecture. About twenty people were there in the center across the way. They listened and we spoke. Afterward there were questions we answered. Open to receive the Turkish people, we found a balance of men and women in the audience. There is an air of spiritual thirst in this part of the world. Turkey, on the cusp of East and West is the gateway from Europe to the Middle East. We were invited to come by a man who knew our work. For the next two weeks this will be our home. We receive the new possibilities in this ancient city. We do not know the future, and we let go of the past. God has us in the *here and now* for a good reason, not always clear in its particulars. The Divine Mother envelopes the city in a blanket of dark. Our bedroom window is illuminated by the streetlights below. The distant horizon has a soft glow as the day is still hanging onto the edge of this eternal urban vista. When the end of the day comes, my mate and I retire together on the bed of holy rest. All the events flash forward in our daily review and we send blessings to our immediate past. In this nocturnal meditation I give myself up to letting go and enter the sleep of preparation for a new day, one of a continual stream of Boundless Mercy.

64

Anger and Conflict

A bomb went off today. Five people in Istanbul were blown up. Many others wounded. We told people to give up anger and conflict forever and BOOM! There it was— a demonstration of anger and conflict on the largest scale, man killing man. A suicide bomber thought God wanted him to do it. "Why not earn my accolades in the afterlife by killing some infidels," he may have said to himself. I am as God created me, as are all other humans in this world. They have their hell they made through free will. Forgiveness gets us out of the hell but who will break the chain of attack thoughts and let go? We were only a few blocks away from the explosion. Some of us heard the blast, and not long after the streets and skies were astir with sirens and helicopters. It was uncanny timing that we would be teaching our students to give up attack, and at that very instant the bomber blew himself up. God said, "Thou shall not kill," and we live to kill. Have we ever really lived? Would one really alive in a state of ecstatic Joy ever think of killing? Dead already. Already people are walking around are dead. We are dead men walking without any notion of who we are as God created us. Peace and Joy abolish attack and killing. They cannot be in the same though system. God and we are Joy and Peace. We are Peace as God created us. The god of killing is a false god of anger and conflict. Let it go and wake up to your true Self. Get out of hell now. Your life is death until you do. Now is the final judgment to accept your peace of Boundless Mercy.

65

The Momentum of Sure Protection

Some days after the Istanbul turmoil, we are relaxing in a restaurant down the street. Some people react and others do not. Peace and safety are internal matters. Suicide bombers are radical for a cause and see conflict and evil everywhere. They are in conflict with Life, with themselves, with the human race. In the cases of the extreme we are a witness to the whole gamut of consciousness. The sub-conscious memories of pain, suffering, and anger are being played out to the max. Killing for a cause is the justification. What "cause" merits killing others who know nothing about it? We are in a war of ideas and these go across borders and societies. A conflict is in the mind of man and played out on the scale of world events. People are killed and injured because of a clash in thought and memories of hurt and revenge. Forgiveness to heal and dissolve the conflict is the only sane approach. We do not know the way to our home free of conflict, but we have called, and God will answer us when we completely let go of our judgments and fears. Heaven is our right, but we must be willing to give it to all. Fearlessness is attaining with open hearts and willing minds to invite the Peace of God beyond our understanding. We are in the flow of grace that releases us from all concerns. We are in the momentum of sure protection that blesses the world with miracles. May our minds be steadfast in the bliss of holy connection. May our hearts contain the multitudes of people deserving Your Boundless Mercy.

66

Nirvana is Always Here

In the middle of Istanbul, we are in the fine restaurant down the street having an early dinner. It is very Americanized. The music is playing in English, and we are relaxed. We are ready for a breakthrough in this town under siege. The bombers bombed, and the people made gestures of fear all around us. The atmosphere is clouded over with the overcast of caution. We observed the gray skies which did not clear for days. The singers sing "let's fall in love" through the speakers in the ceiling. We order our meal and have a sip of wine. The small squares of bread are brought to the table in a miniature brown bag. Oil and balsamic vinegar in a ramekin complement the bread. We enjoy it with the wine, awaiting our main course of salmon and spinach pudding. In this leisurely air of a different world, amidst the tension of terrorism outside, we eat our meal and observe the contrast. How can this revolution be raging when the exact opposite of battle presents itself in our world—peaceful and benevolent to our needs. Which "world" we choose is up to us, and by our thoughts and feelings do we affect or dispel our heaven. Now in this moment is the only "time" there is, and this instant of grace can extend forever to create a world of only happiness. Free will we share with God can choose heaven or make a hell. In Istanbul, the choice is ours here as much as anywhere. We enjoy our meal and our many blessings. Nirvana is always here. Would I be absent? In this Turkish scene of divine providence, we notice the ever-flowing nature of Boundless Mercy.

67

Here and Now

Here and now is the place and time where You abide. No more or less than any other here and now. I can drop all else and come into this presence. Above all else, I can be with You always, in this atmosphere of sacred connection blazing in the awareness of holiness everywhere. What prevents me from joining but my distraction from Your attention? Why would I separate myself from this place in my mind where all problems are solved? It is "time" to put away these diversions into hell, especially when heaven is a decision I can make. In Istanbul as much as any other city, there are forces that govern and define a culture, a city, a group of people congregated together in a particular part of the world. These forces shape all the mood of our encounters here on the bridge between East and West. Asia to the east; Europe to the west. Here we sit together with You on this juncture of Joy. In this juncture of Joy in Istanbul suicide bombers blow themselves up, taking some of the people with them. We remain calm in a building down the street, speaking the virtues of giving up anger forever. Soon the sirens sound and helicopters fly overhead. Out the window I observed a suited man walking nonchalantly across Taksim Square as if nothing had ever happened but the cool breezes blowing in the early spring air. Here and now. Always present amidst the pain and sorrow of an intense human tragedy. Those convinced of the right being more right by killing—an eye for and eye—and those in the forgiving benevolence of Boundless Mercy.

68

What I Need to See

Another long ride in a Turkish taxi going nowhere and in the end fumbling with foreign money and a sleight of hand later, paid five times more than I should. I felt ripped off and I was. Why did I set up this scenario that had all the markings of danger in it? I am not a victim of the world I see, so what is still in me that sets up this unpleasant experience? Perhaps I do not trust. Perhaps I think of lack. Perhaps it is memories of strife in Istanbul from a past life. I am not upset for the reason I think. I am upset because I see something that is not there. Now we have gone to the Four Seasons Hotel in which there is a peace and quiet, insulated from the hawking and squawking of the busy markets and streets. I am coming down from upset, but now I must forgive myself for the replaying of a painful memory. I am not a victim of the circumstances of chaos, so why am I placed in the middle of a mess? Could it be that Americans are hated in this part of the world? When asked, do I need to say I am from Timbuktu? As if I am wearing a sign on my back "easy to take advantage of." I yearn for home. I yearn for safety. I yearn for conditions conducive to Peace. Why place myself in an environment of danger for no reason? I do not need to see more or be more. My tourist days are over. There is nothing I need to see but the peace of God. So even in this unpleasant scene, I ask you Lord to aid me in my escape from thoughts and memories that replay disasters. Place me in the eternal mosque of Boundless Mercy.

69

The True Voice

To have one's own Voice freedom from the known is required. You cannot recite the things learned from another. What is my own discovery? The words of the wise undo my "knowings," and from an emptiness I listen to what comes forth out of that Void. There is an integral relationship between the Void and the true Voice. "I come forth out of the Void into light." Listen for the Unknown that will reveal something true. This "listening" is a reverence, a receptivity to what is coming in. Even the giving meets a need that I may not know exists. A tree gives fruit. What forces consume this fruit? Does the tree concern itself with the "end user"? Most likely that is in the hands of God to determine. The writer writes from this Divine Source, from this Void of true function. What comes forth is the fruit of a Voice directed by the holiness of a truth. It does not have a motive, but it has a very definite shape, texture, taste, and quality that is useful to the Cosmos. It forms a cell in the body of the Divine Mother. It contributes to the whole. I can speak something that contributes to the whole without knowing ahead of time what that contribution will be. That is the future that I leave in the hands of God. A trust comes over me. This utility of what I say is not preplanned, yet I am certain it will have a utility. The oak tree does not calculate the squirrel will use its acorns to get through the winter, yet there is a trust in the tree that every iota of growth is for the perfect extension of Boundless Mercy.

70

What Next

We met an elder lady today. Turkish upper class. She has lived 80 years through the trials of life. Her father was a diplomat, and in that world of refinement, from a family of harmony and happiness. Now she is old, her husband is older by nine years and has given up on life somewhat. A loss in business. An aging body. Friends passed away. What next? With a hearing difficulty, what can be the road to new life, to a restoration of vibrancy? When a person's death urge comes up in old age, it is harder to clear. Almost impossible. He has lost his will to live, so he is suspended in a living "death" in front of the television. Yet she is of a different vibration with the spark of Life and Joy still very much in her core. Those who have a real joy for life never lose it. Those who seem to lose it probably never had it in the first place. Our Lady of Joy had weathered well with a countenance of content. She had seen many come and go. Her own mother lived into her 90s, got a fever one night, and left in the morning with not much ado . . . happy to the very end. So now our Lady is wondering why her husband cannot count his blessings and be more involved with life, with the families of his children, with her. She loves culture and friends. He is withering away in a kind of suspended animation of slow decline. What would infuse her with even more will to thrive and flower? A life of wise encounters could be told and shared. A life that realizes the power of mind to connect with the spirit of immortal life can invoke the forces of Boundless Mercy.

71

India's Embrace

Landed in New Delhi in the early hours. Through the visa control in record speed. Retrieved our bags and went out into the open air to our driver, Narender. Usually he embraces us with open arms, but not this time. Some confusion on our day of arrival. He was not there to greet us. Some feeling of abandonment came over me. We managed to call our friend Retu who arranges things. Within a short while, Narender was on his way. Another hour of waiting added to the last one. He finally arrived and we were off to our hotel. The familiar route came back to us as we drove to the center of town near Connaught Place to our hotel. Greeted by the tall man with a turban and the porters who know us well, we could relax now in the spaciousness of Indian hospitality. We entered the grand lobby sauntering across the smooth expanse of polished marble floors toward the front desk. We felt expanded and connected to the sacredness of India and to the spiritual luxuries it offers. All the past days of uncertainty fade into the present happiness of being well taken care of. The shining faces of the familiar porters greet us, as they take our bags on the trolly and guide us to our room. Up the high-speed elevator to the twenty-second floor, we pass down the hall to our room. A welcome king-sized bed gladly provides our restful comfort. High above the city we can see as far as the hazy atmosphere allows. Birds soar and come to perch outside our window. There is a plate with fruit and some small chocolates on the counter. We each have a chocolate and bite into the taste of Boundless Mercy.

72

The Road to Herakhan

In the mountains, away from it all, we come to sing our praises to the Divine Mother for nine days in Herakhan. On the winding road, we ascend from the bustling Indian town. Higher we go into a more etheric atmosphere as our car takes us closer to Your home of truth, simplicity, and love. We pass through alpine forests on a road lined with an occasional mountain house. People have farms on the terraced side of the slopes. Grains are growing into their golden maturity. Some of the fields have already been harvested. We continue our excursion through the range of peaks that rise from the riverbed below. Closer and closer to our home in Herakhan, we begin to feel the energy emanating from this place of spiritual purity. Babaji is calling us into His realm of certain influence. Gradually we begin to descend to the lower fields just up from the Gautama Ganga River. We see the nine temples on the other side of the massive bed of stones. In the rainy months, the entire riverbed is filled with torrents of water from side to side. Crossing is not possible during this time of the monsoon. But now we are in the dry season. The vegetation can look parched. The road is dusty. Soon we enter the sanctuary of immortal life: Herakhan surrounds us. We are embraced by its potent power of truth, simplicity, and love. Our bags are unloaded and taken to our rooms, carried by young boys eager for a small tip. We arrive in our quarters with a spirit of deep gratitude. Yet again have you granted us Your Boundless Mercy.

73

Worship in Every Action

What worship contains every action of the day? With practice of attention can all my movements and thoughts, deeds, and actions be divine. In the space of a sacred presence the work becomes holy as well. God enters into everything and never leaves. Even in decaying forms is this presence of the divine. In the vibrancy of living things is this flow of energy coming in and out, in a constant exchange with the environments around them. I can be a witness of this divine play. Happy to observe the light upon the leaves which illuminate the various shades of green, and the shoots of chartreuse buds exploding from the branches' ends. The mountain breezes are moving through trees as white birds lite on the rail. The sun is going behind the mountains now, and the orange glow of dusk paints the surfaces of the buildings. We walk to the temple to sing the evening songs to God. The children sitting nearby on the carpet are wide-eyed and alert, moving in a joyous animation that only the very young can do. The hall fills with people—some from the West and some from the Indian cities and villages. The energy builds as the people chant in unison. The drum beats, the bells ring, the harmonium is playing its chords of simple harmony. I smell the incense waft across the atmosphere from the altars. Our friends gather around to increase the voice of gladness being amplified. Each verse increases the divine presence of one Mind as we follow the Sanskrit words that express our devotion. What could be the song of Life that sings itself constantly? This model of sounds expresses your Boundless Mercy.

74

An Essential Correction

On the mountainside of Dehradun overlooking the valley in early evening, I bask in the appreciation of true friends who have helped me through a health crisis. A long-standing condition now corrected and their support above and beyond normal hospitality made possible this correction. Now in recovery at their home, Annapurna, the pain of surgical procedures subsiding, I am in the first urge to express this essential event. The body takes on the negative conditions of thoughts in the subconscious memory bank and manifests a disease. Sometimes it has gone so far as to need a drastic intervention to turn it around. In my case, the pressures of daily life made a chronic condition requiring surgery to correct. My resistance to accept help made the condition worsen. Finally, my friends insisted I handle the problem. With their support I found the right doctor and hospital to have the surgery. They even handled the bill so I could pay them later. It was a trial, but I faced my fears and surrendered. Babaji arranged it with His infinite grace. The procedures went well, and I was only in the hospital for two days. I had done the right thing for my health, and my friends and wife were by my side the whole way. The doctor was an expert and had compassion. All worked together in a dance of perfection. Only one night did I endure intense pain but even then, the modern medications knocked me out so I would not be in agony long. I cleared a lot of past-life war around memories. Now I overlook the dusk on the mountain and thank the Lord for his blessing of Boundless Mercy.

75

What Grace This Is

I am in a haven from the world. I am in a sanctuary of perfect hospitality. I am the receiver of immense grace amidst the mountains of Dehradun. My friends have cared for me better than I could have cared for myself. My wife has showered me with love and care. What grace is this freely bestowed on me? What forces are behind this perfect action of healing? Can I rise to meet all that has been given me? What do I have to give in return to express my true appreciation? God moves us into situations that provide the lessons we need to awaken. People come into our sphere of influence to uplift and enlighten us to greater heights of heaven on earth. I feel humbled by this level of love that comes to me unasked, as I bow my head in the aura of divine providence. The serene shapes of mountains rise in the distance to form a chain of crests linked together in a dramatic horizon. The sun sets on the plains and illuminates the slopes with a brilliant warmth. Shadows lengthen in the coming dusk. The birds lodge in the nearby trees to prepare for their night of rest. In the living area of this holy home, the television is on with the Western news. Reporters do their reports on the state of affairs around the world. A cooing dove on the veranda speaks her own report—a song of wellbeing, unbeknownst of the "news." Universal sounds pay no heed to the man-made clamor. I choose to listen and look to the heaven of my true surroundings. Why would I disrupt this perfection with the wars of time when I can inhabit the timeless peace of creation? In this perfect sanctuary of hospitality, I receive the flow of Boundless Mercy.

76

A Sacred Scenario

It is morning here in Dehradun, and I am up as the sun rises over the crests of mountains that form the long purple grey line of sentinels. A cow speaks her sounds into the atmosphere from the estate below. The ceiling fan throws its breeze into the living room, rustling the newspaper that rests on the end of the coffee table. On the hour, the clock chimes. I observe a peace of mind that envelops this place of early awakenings. Rich aromas from the kitchen waft into the delight of this sensual Shangri-La. God moves immensely in the little things which orbit my awareness. These compose the constellations of harmonious combinations. These form relationships essential to life. These make up my magnificent menagerie of holy artifacts, my collection of compassionate kernels of common truths. The wooden table takes on monumental proportions as it stands stalwart upon the marble slabs of flooring. The bricks are laid into rows upon rows, forming the basic structure of this home. In this spacious living room of sanctuary, I look out upon the veranda that wraps around the entire house. The sun brightens as the atmosphere takes on a haze. The temperature increases as I appreciate more and more the protection of the shade. A bamboo chime makes melodious sounds in the sway from a breeze. The relaxation of divine leisure envelops the environment with an energy of complete appreciation. Not just from me, but between these holy things which compose this sacred scenario, a gratitude emerges among the molecules of matter that make up the table and chime, the cow and clock, the marble and the mountains. I am at the crossroads of these collective combinations, observing their contributions of Boundless Mercy.

77

Home and Ultimate Home

Our circuitous travels always lead back to home. It is not merely a place, but a state of rest in God that puts aside all tasks and actions in order to make contact with the stillness and silence that contains everything. This real home is not determined by conditions, yet when order is most present and attentive, the stillness and silence is most noticeable. These are always there, but our attentions direct us to elsewhere. Some of these diversions are necessary, but for their transmutation back to home. The journey is always to bring greater parameters to this home. Why not? When all things are brought into heaven, where is there room for hell? When all people are brought home, who is a stranger here? We catch up with local news and speak with our friends. All is good in the re-entry process. We get our rest and deep sleep to restore us to an energy of fresh newness. The Indian classical music blesses our house with cosmic sounds of peace and joy unparalleled in the oeuvre of world compositions. The musician saints pluck their notes on the instruments of universal possibilities. Each musical phrase is a balm to my soul—a healing sound that transcends all discordant sounds of conflict and strife. My mind is brought to silence. I wish to be free of all thoughts but God's. Even in these moments of deep appreciation for home, I can go one more step closer to this portal to Truth. The movement through to the other side of human reason is not possible through understanding. My home of the Unknown is immensely more benevolent than my paltry constructs of time. In this reflection of my ultimate home, I have forgiven what I see and what I do. Even the mistakes of future wanderings are afore forgiven in this sanctuary of Boundless Mercy.

78

In the Momentum of Peace

A morning in Florida at a back-alley café in Delray Beach, we have a small breakfast and listen to the plane fly overhead. Sparrows chirp in the palms and hop up to the table looking for crumbs. Two ladies converse and share pictures of their grandchildren on their iPhones. An azure firmament free of clouds spans overhead. We eat an omelet and some fresh fruit with a cup of coffee on the side in a paper cup. Soon we are finished with this small repast and rise to return to our hotel, leaving behind a few tidbits for the sparrows, scattered around the table on the brick pavement. We walk the short distance to the Marriott across the main thoroughfare, Atlantic Avenue. Soon we are sauntering down the opulent hallways across the marble floors that are polished to a high sheen. The grand lobby is spacious and inviting with numerous areas to sit. I marvel at a sand sculpture of the hotel in the middle of a rotunda, directly under a massive chandelier. Some diligent hands formed it with love; my appreciation grows for their quiet artistry. As we ascend to our room in the glass-side elevator, a sense of height comes upon us as we observe the floor levels pass by. Our room is a spacious haven overlooking the ocean side. A dense row of palm trees grows parallel to the beach, protecting the buildings from the sea breezes. This morning in Florida produces a perfect leisure. I am in the momentum of a peace that surrounds me in this tropical haven of southern Boundless Mercy.

79

These Elemental Blessings

In the ancient world now of Greece on the island of Hydra. Sitting by the perfect horseshoe bay having our morning coffee in the shade of the expansive canopy, we have our conversation with friends from Athens. The bright morning sun shines on the boats that crowd against the docks. Our breakfast arrives and we savor the well-prepared omelets. There is a leisure on this island enhanced by the absence of cars or buses. Only pedestrians pass by, or an occasional donkey carrying goods to the hotels and homes on the hills. Tourists come to bask in the picturesque tranquility of this seaside town of ancient origins. We are but observers of this scenario of beauty in this Mediterranean vision of an era outside of time. These are seafaring people who set the stage for Western culture. In the mainland city of Athens, a culture congealed and spread across the Western countries. Italy first, then through Rome and all the rest. Yet here in Hydra are the seeds of a way of life. The building blocks of culture present themselves here. The center of town is for commerce; people gather and visit the shops. They catch their boats back to Athens and disembark from the same. As we finish eating our food, an appreciation engulfs my mind for all that is given. Peace and quiet are always here as the elements nurture and provide for the human race. Earth, sky, water come together in a perfect blend. The town of stone buildings and streets grow out of these elemental blessings. For all we know, this simplicity is the heart of Boundless Mercy.

80

The Holy Halo of Truth and Beauty

Apollo, the God of Light, is honored in Delphi. We travel from Athens to Delphi by car, across the Grecian landscape into the mountain region of Parnassus. On the mountain roads that wind through spectacular vistas, we prepare ourselves to meet the sacred. The ancient site of Delphi housed the Oracle, the wise woman in touch with Divine inspiration, directly from the Light, a true channel of Apollo. She sat over the crevasse. Up from the bowels of the Earth came a gas that put her in a trance. Then from the etheric realms did she speak in tongues of truth the wisdom which shaped the ages. From far and wide did kings bow at her feet to receive divine directions. "Know thyself" was uttered in true force. Delphi grew up as the navel of the Earth, the place of cosmic community where diverse peoples joined in whole rejoicing to honor their common good, to praise the God of Light that brings life to all things. In the midst of these lofty vibrations we walk the grounds of history, yet in the present still is the holy halo of truth and beauty forming a vast firmament surrounding and emanating an energy of magnificence. We stand by the entrance to the Temple of Apollo in awe of the vertical columns which guide us upward to the heavens. In the theater, we gain perspective from above to see the full plan of this temple that housed the Oracle. Listening to the channel of truth, we hear a rare gem of sacred statement: "Beauty is your connection to Source." In this is Boundless Mercy.

81

The Navel of the Earth

At the spring in Delphi, the Oracle's nectar bursting eons ago from deep within the Earth, I and my companions take a long drink. Nourished with the cool, the taste of ancient wisdom on or lips, we saunter to the shady place under the canopy of the foliage forming a green dome of cathedral-like proportions. In this sacred space of reverence, we breathe in the atmosphere that charged this place a millennium ago, and still imbues the very air with holiness. We are on this pilgrimage to the spirit that still lives in this city of God. What matters of the names and shapes of things when man looks upward to the glory of his Creator? Overhead is a firmament of new spring leaves that shades us from the brightness of the sun. The sound of flowing streams forms the music in the background as our voices speak of gratitude and awe. The dome of Parnassus towers overhead and forms a natural amphitheater that cradles this eternal site in the lap of Mother Earth. Massive are the walls of wonder that boggle the mind to fathom the origins of this place. Truly the Hand of God was upon it through the hearts and minds of its creators. And Zeus himself sent eagles to converge and mark the spot on which the navel of the Earth emerges. From there Apollo's light made clear its holy charge, as gods came down to Earth and made their presence known. O, Greeks of old who sang their praises to the heights of reason, would not your notes of gracious homage live on in Boundless Mercy.

82

Awake in Our True Nature

In Barcelona, the pace of leisure is the norm. Streets have wide walkways, and some are down the middle with cafes and flower vendors amidst the traffic on both sides. Trees form a canopy for shade extending for blocks into the distance. The sky is crisp—a sharp blue, with no clouds, contributing to a clear atmosphere of brilliant light. We enter the café near our residence and have our morning breakfast. People gather with their friends for lively conversation. The local pastry is displayed in the glass cases for the people to choose. Hot chocolate is served like pudding—thick and strong in ceramic cups. We spoon it up in delight, listening to the Spanish being spoken. A different energy abides in Spain. More relaxation is in the culture. Less pressure to produce. More ability to enjoy simple living. Strong family values. People like to congregate in cafes and take a time out from business. We have our coffee and crescent as we write in our books. My consort and I give ourselves this space to be free of concerns. Happiness is the reason for being, Joy is the nature of Life. What is not pure Joy is only a dream. This time in Barcelona is our chance to be in the universal flow of being awake in our true nature. It does not matter what we do, so long as it is happy. Striving is finished when the present extends into the future. We sit in the cafe and feel the presence of gratitude. Completing our stay in Spain, Barcelona makes its impression in this world journal of Boundless Mercy.

83

Clarity

Stockholm, a northern town, water all around, in a two-story flat with a lot of space. Friends come, and some who need clarity in their lives. An older gem, a friendship formed three decades back, in the foreign ministry of government now, brought us to this place of new entry. A Swedish community, here the help is needed, comes to heal through the breath. We meet in the lofty apartment of our friend and call in a psychic one who is clearly connected with the higher realms. Decades ago, a first meeting of minds took place, exchanges made, hearts joined, souls put together for exceptional clarity. "Your mind is like a crystal," she said to my consort. Thirty years hence still the same---minds even more clear in their present communion. Red is the color of love giving in abundance. Blue is the pillar of light restoration. Throat chakra made clear by blue. Words come to me. I am into words through a crown wide open. Perhaps too wide open I would need protection to keep the integrity of my receptions clear. No big deal—ask Babaji to protect; Jesus to forgive; Divine Mother to blanket with tenderness and care. The psychic channel is strong, from the second friend who is close to the first. Fields and forests of green come around me for restoration. I connect with the truth of the moment, with the messages that come through the spirit realm. A journey to a new level in which the energy of life flows through me in greater amounts of Joy. In this Swedish moment of reception, I am taken to a clarity for strength—your Boundless Mercy.

84

The Blue Lagoon of Transformation

Iceland now, a short flight from Stockholm, near the Blue Lagoon. Amidst the dark, jagged rocks of lava fields, mossy covered with lime green, it seems a human form in this setting somewhat out of place, an element too ephemeral in this solid spread of volcanic grounding. I could accept my presence in this expanse of elemental power. The aqua blue waters of the lagoon wash over me. I go into an altered state of suspended animation where my mind is paramount; it connects me to the cosmos. Within these waters where I float in bliss would I let go of more worldly concerns and call in a new vision of my purpose here. What fills the canvas of my life? How would I paint it? What subjects appear to me in this invocation of heavenly direction? I invite the unseen to present itself. What Unknown Forces are working here in this Nordic crucible of change? In these summer months of the midnight sun, the brilliance of day extends itself past the usual dusk of my history and puts me in the present glory of new vastness I feel in these fields of volcanic expansion. The jagged edges of the black rock meet the milky aqua blue of the Divine Mother's bath of certain cleansing. It is not only my body which is cleaned in this thermal bath of change, but my mind as well is cleared of doubt and discontent. I go into this Blue Lagoon of transformation and come out of it in a different light, in a new divine space more connected to my Source, more aware of my surroundings, more unified with the people I call friends, and the people I do not call my friends in this Icelandic realm of Boundless Mercy.

85

Sanctuary of Sacred Natural Elements

Northern light surrounds this land of Vikings and fields of volcanic black rock. What ancient urge to explore these remote island lands of Iceland brought them so far from home? How many years did it take them to establish a colony which sustained the people who came along in the ships, not knowing what or how or when they would ever return to the familiar shores of Denmark or other Nordic homelands? I am here now, after centuries have passed and a country has formed around the heritage of these early exploring souls. Jet planes bring tourists from other counties to see the wonders of natural beauty. Glaciers of ice and volcanoes of fire cohabitate the landscape. Fish is the food of the day, most every day. The waters of the Blue Lagoon have been prepared for the foreign guests to come by the hundreds to fill the thermal waters with an international crowd of pleasure seekers. In the waters as well, I float and let my mind wander. An inner world do I see when I take a deep breath and allow its release. The atmosphere of Iceland is alive, charged with the explosive potential of the land. The people too have this nature of focus, this endeavor to make a colony established. Yet, in its own right, a country now not beholding to a former land of fathers and mothers. Iceland, in this very northern sea of isolation, you draw the multitudes toward this feeling of escape, this sanctuary of the sacred natural elements that imbue their Boundless Mercy.

86

The Balinese Goddesses

As much as one can be present with the very things around, in whatever setting of a humble or grand nature, there is a mixture of palpable sensations with the recent recollections of impressions and encounters. I write in my apartment in West End, Nashville, which is not only comforting and spacious in my view but filled with the objects that have their abilities to transport my mind to other worlds. For instance, the elongated goddesses from Bali—at home in the rice fields—now find themselves hanging in our living room on the northeast wall. All by themselves, the three pillars of holiness with hands in prayer hold the space to stop the minds of those who have the eyes to see. They pray with hands together, clasped and held close to their solar plexus, slightly tilted forward, in a row of three—one tallest first, then the shorter two after in a kind of mini-procession. Queenly in their stature, they all are crowned with head dresses that appear as plump orbs flanked by two prongs, or even horns, that point upwards. This verticality is strong; stronger than El Greco's elongated bodies, as vertical as Giacometti's tall standing men, and akin to Barnett Newman's vertical stripe, these Balinese goddesses gather together for the benefit of our spiritual aspiration. There is an order in these physical planes that would forget about all that matters except this one thing—our drive to aspire upward to places yet unknown, yet unseen and unfelt, yet certainly broader, deeper, higher, and more beautiful than the mixture of "good and evil" we find in worldly life. To this the goddesses take us in Boundless Mercy.

87

Kitchen Counter Pondering

Again, I come back after a long pause, to write these beatitudes of grace. Another circle of travel is complete. This time in the southern and western regions of these United States. Back in Nashville, at our kitchen counter with my cup of coffee in the morning hours. I jot down a few words. Our life is simplified. Our home is free of clutter. One can relax and escape the constant activity of the world. I observe my wife preparing food for the afternoon meal. The lights overhead illuminate this page to receive Your blessings. To what ends do I apply our days? Are we adoring our existence? What reasons are present in my mind to be glad, if not the many objects of beauty that surround me into infinity? Each thing has tremendous grace to impart. All our modern gadgets are at our fingertips: iPhone, laptop, refrigerator, coffee maker, which give our world facility. Electricity flows through them to make them work. Electricity from the Cosmos flows through us to make us work. What is this Life Force that manifested a Cosmos? It's something big and powerful, and at the same time, miniscule and gentle. It forms an ocean and a droplet of water. It forms a Mount Everest and a grain of sand. It forms a sun and millions of suns to make up a galaxy. It goes out through the space of infinite galaxies It is mighty massive. All this I ponder at my kitchen counter, drinking my cup of brew. All this comes to me in a palpable observation, on this morning at home in Boundless Mercy.

88

The Joy of Life

There is hope that the Joy of life will dominate my mind without much effort, without much ado. In the simple acknowledgements, a gratitude sweeps over me. I take a deep breath and touch upon a gladness within. I feel the pen in my hand and appreciate the ease of the ink flowing upon the page, and notice the beauty of the paper, the leather binding of the book made in Italy. I step into the shower for my morning cleanse and appreciate all the complex systems of engineering that deliver clean water to my door. "Mine eyes have seen the Glory of the coming of the Lord." It is in the simple things of Life through which the Lord in His glory is seen. When you are looking for your own happiness, which is your rightful divine inheritance, you will find it. When your mind wanders into problems, doubt, depression, and negative "proofs" of how "bad" things are in the world, you will get more of "that." The Glory of the Lord is in His one-pointed ability and determination to see only Joy. He looks upon the contradictions to joy as mere tests, as mirages to be dismissed as having no real substance. The illumination that comes with a decision to be happy sheds light on everything you see, because seeing now emanates from the heart of Love whose messengers are Peace and Joy. Joy is Glory. To see joy in the coffee cup and the leisure time to relax in the delight of drinking your cup of coffee is to see the Glory of the Lord coming into all aspects of your everyday life. In this awareness one is free, basking in the gifts of Boundless Mercy.

89

Love of Self

The person we really need to love in this life is our Self. We experience so many ups and downs and victories and defeats, it would be easy to withdraw from the game of Life in a self-imposed exile. Sometimes the first thought of our day is not one of world-shaking elation, but rather a mild form of dread. How to get out of this? The universal forces do all that they can to bring us to Joy. And it is helpful to define these forces as benevolent to us—not against our pursuit of happiness in any way. Our time is now to be in this flow of good tidings. I like to sit in the morning and connect with them. We play some uplifting songs of celebration in our house, just after our shower, making the bed, brewing the first pot of coffee. They are in Sanskrit, so I can connect with the uplifting nature of the tunes without knowing the meaning. There is only one meaning, really, that of divine adoration and gratitude. Gratitude is a great eraser of the doldrums. One need not go far to find reasons for appreciation; just the fact of running water in our households is cause for Joy when one considers how many humans live without this basic necessity. In our house we have some beautiful things: oriental carpets, a carved wood trunk with Chinese figures, sculptures of saints from India, paintings of the Divine Mother, etc. One needs the space in the morning to appreciate one's surroundings and the good fortune of an orderly life. In this space we can connect with the inner feelings of goodness that define our higher nature. In this connection is the Love of Self that we so much need. To love yourself is Boundless Mercy.

90

A Living Teacher of Life

A living teacher of Life is not so easy to find. There are a lot of phony gurus who have motives other than the right one—to liberate the student from falseness of thought, word, deed, and action. When a person does blunder into a real teacher, there is a certainty that this meeting was pre-ordained to take place. This is the most blessed encounter in life. The light of true reason is transmitted from the teacher to the student. Henceforth, the student is never the same after that transmission, even though it may take him years to integrate what he has received. This is how eternal wisdom is passed down. Books can contain an explanation of important principles, but without their coupling with this actual flesh and blood relationship, the principles remain just ideas, untested in the crucible of actual Life encounters and relationships. I met Tara Singh in 1989 during an Easter retreat. My life was eternally altered from that meeting. What did it do? What did he say that changed me so drastically? you may ask. He undid everything I thought I knew in about the first five minutes. He moved me out of the relative knowledge of opposites—good vs. bad—into the Absolute knowledge free of opposites, in which only peace and compassion abide. He got me to "let go" of my opinions and judgments that composed my false self. He brought my own thought to silence so deep within me that I surrendered my whole past at his feet. A living teacher of Life is worth more than anything or anyone else, even parents. A living teacher of Life is a font of Boundless Mercy.

91

Technology

We live in a technological world of cars, computers, appliances, and amenities at our fingertips. Almost every aspect of our life is covered by an app. Tech support is almost synonymous with Divine Help. When the phone doesn't work, we go through major anxiety. What if we can't be reached? Who needs to be reached? Communication is a major aspect of our daily life. Emails come through the ethers to those who are connected. Nearly all of us are. What are we communicating? What happens to us when we are not "online"? Today, our phone went "dead," so I am writing about this. We still have internet, so I can post this on Facebook, but what do we have to say to one another regardless of the technology which has become synonymous with "communication"? If "The holy spirit speaks through me today," as Jesus says in Lesson #296 of A Course in Miracles, what am I to speak? The content of the message is different from the medium through which the message is delivered. Technology is not the content; it is just the means. What is the end? Are we in a state or pure Joy, happiness, unconditional Love, Heaven on Earth? Or do we fall into the moods and minds of discontent, anger, irritation, depression, unhappiness? Are we claiming our Heaven or asserting our hell? The devices we use cannot determine the actual state of heart and soul in which we abide. That is up to us, and this decision is independent of technology without the fears of having "no phone service." I am still connected to Boundless Mercy.

92

Dreams and Awakening

This is the day after my birthday, November 12, and the day before we leave for Australia. The universe is expanding and unfolding according to Cosmic Law. Joy is still the highest vibe that manifests reality. The wise say "there are no problems in Life." That is the same as saying only the Joy of God exists. All else are "dreams." They are erroneous thoughts of fear projected onto the Life stream, making up such things as pain, sorrow, and death. A dream, as we know, is not real. It is a projected image in our mind, often structured in accordance with our neurotic fears which disappear when we "wake up." In the dream, all seems to be real, yet once we awaken it is clear the dream was a fantasy. Problems are in the dream of waking life—still a "waking dream." Enlightenment is full awakening. It is the freedom from deceptions that "seem so real" in the waking dream. Problems seem so real when we are in them. What solves them or dissolves them? We need a different perspective that is fully awake. What would wake us up? First, see that *I am the projector of the dream of the problems.* Then, *I can stop the projector by admitting I am the maker of problems.* And then, *total forgiveness and letting go of the thoughts in the dream, and then allowing the feelings of Joy that result from this freedom.* On this day after my birthday—Armistice Day—I call an end to the dream of war and claim the Joy of Boundless Mercy.

93

Water, This Sacred Element

The atmosphere of rain is here in Bali this time of year. Every day a cloudburst comes in the afternoon. Sheets of rain fall from nowhere it seems then cease in the early evening time. We sit in the dining veranda of our villas having an afternoon coffee, listening to the droplets hitting the lush vegetation. A slight breeze blows. The sound of passing cars and motorbikes whizz by in the distance. Thunder rumbles its base notes as the downpour quickens, making the sound of rain louder and louder. A light mist comes toward us from the outside as we watch the storm grow in proportion. Water streams come down from the thatched rooves forming vertical lines of steady drops. All the foliage is laden with the unending moisture soaking up the holy nectar of a life sustaining deluge. A sharper thunder cuts through the sky from a different direction behind us. Slowly the volume of rain lessens, as we await a lull in the storm which allows us to return to our villa. A natural cycle completes itself to begin again tomorrow. Now I hear the running water of the fountain below, put there by the hands of men yet singing the song of this sacred element. Water everywhere, we could not live without You. Divine Mother, who meets our needs, brings forth this liquid Love to cleanse us and bless us, composing our bodies with this sacred substance. Give us gratitude for the deluge, for the rains that impart Your Boundless Mercy.

94

Care Verging on Divine Dedication

I am in Bali again for the sixth time, each visit deeper than the last. At Nefatari Villas we have a family of Balinese who take care of us in all aspects of our stay. Their care is beyond mere hotel service, verging on a divine dedication that is common in the Balinese culture. Before cleaning our room in the morning, sacred offerings are made to clear the atmosphere as well. A young woman came this morning to make them, and she looked like a goddess—so pure and serene. Could you imagine this in the West? All over Bali people place God at the top of their daily purpose, so their "first thought" is worship. It is their work of the day to honor the divine. The young woman came into our villa with a woven tray of offerings—each in a small woven grass basket of its own with flowers and sticks of burning incense. She placed one small basket of buds and petals by the pool. I watched the smoke of the incense stick waft upwards above the turquoise water of our pool as the lady moved like a dancer toward the covered veranda. There did she stop before a small altar built out from the wall. Offering flowers with various hand gestures, time stopped in my observance of this profound beauty of her sacred movements. A blanket of peace came over me; a light of pure gratitude emanated from my heart into the space surrounding our villa. This girl of the Goddess expressed only the truth of Boundless Mercy.

95

Joy is the Sister of Peace

In this open-air dining area of Nefatari we are above the gardens below. Much peace abounds in the vegetation. The plumeria blooms are bursting out in hot pink. The evening is descending upon the land as sounds slow down and the water runs in the fountain in the courtyard below, filling the atmosphere with a constant gurgle. I order a beer—Bintang—brewed in Indonesia. When I am still and disengaged from activity, I can hear the truth of this present Joy. The relaxation in Bali is profound, as a wave of appreciation comes over me. My consort and I have our meal together with our other guests in the divine leisure of deepest ease and calm. I can hear the subtle sounds of forks touching the plates and soft conversation lending to the gentle crescendo of laughter. Joy is the sister of Peace—sometimes expressed in the rain, sometimes in the sound of thunder, sometimes sitting at the dinner table sipping a cold beverage. At the forefront of this present moment I can receive it. From thee I sing, pure Joy of the present, in all my observations and statements of observations. Whatever you have in store for me in my future, I place in Your hands. Gods bow down to You, sister of Peace. You answer only to Love, Your Father, and the entire Cosmos, Your Mother. In Bali you are so close to me in these sublime villas. I weave myself into Your offerings of this day and all its happenings that parade before me in this action of Boundless Mercy.

96

Home in Bali's Burst of Absolute Beauty

This afternoon is hot and humid in the December days of Bali. Sweating is natural for those of us not used to this climate. I am on the veranda of our villa, outside the air-conditioned bedroom, sitting at our wonderful teak breakfast table drawing and writing as I listen to the Beatles on my wireless headphones. Two of us in Bali form a complete nirvana. We are on our way home to our real home of heaven on Earth. Perhaps people say this place does not exist. but they are wrong. The elements in this island in Indonesia can line up in such a way that we experience a Garden of Eden, a Valhalla of harmony, a home of the most profound spiritual reality. Memories of where our true Self dwells come rushing back to us. What is inside is outside; peace within is seen as peace without. Rice patties and well-placed vegetation in our villas provide a verdant truth. All the green in Bali heals us of our scarcity thoughts of unnatural limitation. We can easily correct ourselves in this Bali Burst of Absolute Beauty. Yes, there is Western influence which has tainted this island with the disease of industrialized society, yet even with this influence there is an impeccable innocence which prevails in the land, the people, the practices of Divine adoration. We are on our way home to heaven, my consort and I, the two of us standing erect in the graciousness of Bali's certain holiness. We are going home for sure to the core of our Being in this land of Boundless Mercy.

97

Among the Ministers of God

The sun is out today in Bali, which is rare in the rainy season. Young men are here cleaning our villa when we return from breakfast. There is a sacred aura in their movements, harmoniously working together to bring complete order to all aspects of our place. They sweep up the fallen leaves from the floor of the courtyard and use a net on a pole to strain the debris which has fallen into the pool. The bed is made with clean sheets in the most impeccable way. Two young men draw the sheets tightly across the king bed after drawing up the veils that form the sheer canopy encircling this sanctuary of rest. Not a wrinkle remains when in the completed makeover. The bed takes on a new vibration—a touch from God through the hands of these young men. Similarly, the bathroom is cleansed with this divine attention. As quietly as they came, the smiling young cleaning crew leaves the place totally restored to impeccability. There is an aftermath of silence in the atmosphere because of their presence which amounts to nothing short of a divine invocation. Their cleaning calls in the gods, and with this call comes a blanket of peace that descends and covers our place. It is so palpable one can feel it and hear it. Even the sweet smell of the flowers and incense make a lasting impression in our minds. We are among the ministers of God with the Balinese attendants who make our world here at Nefatari Villas a Shangri-La, a heaven on Earth. In this place we experience the grace of Boundless Mercy.

98

An Honored Guest

We await our guest who has traveled across skies to our home. Modern means plummet us through space at almost the speed of sound. We fly better than birds in our intercontinental trajectories. She has touched down and now is in a cab, coming our way. We wait with the excitement of anticipation. The guest is the one who brings God's graces into our home. We are the beneficiary of this influx of goodness. It awakens the elation that sits waiting to come pouring out of us. It primes the pump of our eternal spring flowing gifts of living water to the thirsty, caring for the guest hospitably, returning same done for us in foreign lands. Gloriously we wait until the text comes, "I am here." At the front door waiting, with us almost running to greet, to hug, to catch up on the news. Opening our home, opening our hearts, opening our capacity to give and receive, opening the new year with a guest of huge proportions. What do we have to give? This is the only real question we need to ask ourselves in life. Inspired to take care of another, who are we? What is our purpose here except for that? Our guest arrived and we went to dinner nearby. We paid the bill with a gladness in our hearts. Shared stories of common bonds, common friends, common experiences around the world. We talked into the night. We watched the news together on the late-night TV. Surely the recipients of Boundless Mercy.

99

Love's Messengers

We have the words of the wise from the past whose impact in the present depends on our attention to them. Why do we communicate with words if not to uplift and make happy? Is not the essence of wisdom true Love? If "philosophy" means "love of wisdom," and true wisdom is merely love, then the real philosopher is "in love with love." Each philosopher worth his/her salt in the annals of human contributions is focused on the increase of Love upon the planet. With a propensity for words—for using words to make clear the "increase of love upon the planet"—the real philosopher walks with saints. Saints may not express through words their "increase of love," but act in direct relationships with those they meet in life. Love clarifies the words of the philosopher and inspires the actions of the saints. Both are Love's messengers. Those who have mastered the understanding and action of Love are beautiful. This mastery is the lifeblood that keeps their memory alive. We remember Jesus and Plato because they transformed the purpose for living. "Love ye one another" and "know thyself" have been the eternal messages of the wise. But now we have to live like them and bring their good memory into the present. He who lives by the words and actions of the philosophers and saints becomes as they are—a saint himself in application of their principles. Storms and turns of fate cannot affect the one aligned with a universal truth. As above, so below in the order of the cosmos, permeating a vast and infinite space while every celestial body formed in Boundless Mercy.

100

The Content of Consciousness

We are on the eve of departure. There are things to pack and get together. We watched Krishnamurti discuss the emptying out of consciousness through the overall observation of thought and its nature. Incarnation into the continuity of thought perpetuates the age-old conflicts, fears, insecurities, and problems. Is it possible to "die" to thought, to see the pernicious nature of its total content? The brain is the storehouse of memory, the governor of the body. Is it possible to transcend the brain and thought all together? Not through analysis or a psychological theory, but through an act of true renunciation. Can we look at the whole content of consciousness, even the vast subconscious part and totally step out of it? Why would we want to? Freedom, Love, Beauty, Immortality exist outside the field of the known—the content of consciousness. A real incarnation into Life requires a "death," a departure from this field of the known. It is a radical shift. Few are willing to even ponder the wisdom of this action. The fear of death prevents us from examining it. We deal with it emotionally when it comes to us in the death of a parent or family member, but we do not really plumb the depths of it in our life, and its relationship to Energy. The "death" of thought is not its destruction, but the ending of our attachment to it. The immortality of Love and Beauty come to us free of time, free of problems, free of thought in a state of Boundless Mercy.

101

The Cycle of Return

The cycle of return, yet to go out again, I sit in our kitchen awaiting the coffee to brew. What is there to say and write when the silence is so satisfying? What foray into action merits the motion when stillness is supreme? My wife pours the coffee and adds a little cream. She brings it to me as I write these words of thanks. Putting on her coat, she tells me of her morning errands, then opens the front door and is gone. I hear footsteps as heels hit the floor in the apartment above. A sip of coffee is like morning nectar. The fan of the furnace comes on and blows warm air through the ducts. On a winter day in February I can appreciate this shelter—more of a sanctuary of sacredness---which surrounds me with a home. But the real home is not a place, it is a peace within, a being that I accept as mine, joined with all other beings who share this life. What is this cycle of return that feels like a completion yet takes a journey onward to new vistas, new shelters, new encounters with people not yet met? I ponder the reason to be. Would joy be sustained even amid change and uncertainty? I will go out again to where? The home I have now is always my sanctuary of sanity. It is the silence of an all-pervading love, the stillness of every object of adoration speaking of its own beauty and poise. What need have I to fear when God's peace and joy are mine? We return only to the Source of our Self, which we never really left. What journey is left to take but this one? It is a giant leap into the Presence of who we are in Boundless Mercy.

102

On the Verge of a Move

On the verge of a move. On the tail end of a long stay in Nashville—eight years. Near perfect accommodations graced us through the Masters' blessings. All things provided within a three-block radius. No car needed. Now off to our nation's capital to take our stand for Liberation—one nation under God, with liberty and justice for all. Which is to say peace and joy for all. Joy is the real justice that transcends the bonds of conflict. Love is the Law of the Land which abolishes fear. What is for some is for all. We the People are One Entity. To care for our Self is to make certain all are cared for. Moving into the Unknown energy toward a meeting with my fate, my destiny. What is in store for these future moments of following You? Love is aware of the present and trustful of a future placed in the hands of God. I am at a branching in the road: the one looks left to comfort, to calculated routines already maintaining survival, the one to the right is outside my comfort zone, filled with new possibilities yet to be realized, in need of miracles to be made manifest. I choose the second. I choose the Unknown. I choose to trust in the directions we have received from above which were planted in our souls from long ago. My life is Yours to guide today. Let me be glad and rejoice in it. Let me move in fearlessness that Love will provide everything in Her action of Boundless Mercy.

103

A Long-Awaited Guest

Awaiting a guest, long awaited, it seems. All this time in Nashville and at the end of our tenure here she emerges. People came and went, as usual, but this one different. Perhaps after eating the fish and bread she will stay. What trap is this personality we all maintain in its contrivances to triumph over the God-created Self? The world is a place people make up themselves with an image. Even one with a spiritual inclination. Who can be free of images and meet the world disenthralled from making up a self? No need to make up what is only perfect. She comes with child anew, a mother in her first year, perhaps this is the reason for her freedom—discovering the one thing to give. A new life upon the planet out of her body, out of her soul, which requires a new attention, a constant caring for one who is helpless. Pure joy at her breasts, a function of the Divine Mother of universal proportions. There are things that the Cosmos created. Of these I sing, of the mother and child, of the place we must rest, of the new movement toward the new city Washington, of the friends who came and the friends gone by, of the action toward freedom, of the chains of limitation left behind, of the skies above through which we travel, of the lands upon which we set our feet. The guest, the most sacred, having come from heaven sent, now in our life. I send out my prayer for permanence—what comes over the horizon is here to stay. The guest is an eternal blessing now, filling our hearts forever new with Boundless Mercy.

104

Perfection Everywhere

On the island of St. Croix on the eastern-most outpost of the US, drinking a club soda with lemon wedge in a seaside café. The warm breeze comes into the dining room through the open façade and I sit relaxed, appreciating my leisure. Babaji moves us around on the game board of the Earth's many places. Some in the middle of a continent, others in the middle of an ocean. In the West Indies now for the first time, I observe the culture of not much to do. Leisure verges on the edge of laziness. People want the long beaches of palm trees and aqua waters to give them a respite from their pressures or to warm them for two weeks in the middle of harsh northern winters. It is a "time out," a suspended animation, a "lay-around-doing-very-little" culture. Tourists come here to escape. People move here to escape. There is an air of disrepair in the atmosphere. An island life can be one of poverty. Faces staring as we drive by the end of the block. Dark black faces, some happy and in their power and proud of who they are, others downtrodden and lethargic in a stupor of dysfunction. Driving over the rough roads we are jostled and shaken in our journey to our home. We stop to fill the radiator with water in the old jalopy. Palm groves seem to pass us as we drive over the narrow highway. A well of gratitude comes from different places now—not in the observed—but in the awareness of perfection everywhere. It is with the stillness and silence of Boundless Mercy.

105

A Pax Britannia

A week in the United Kingdom began with a sky of blue with gentle puffs of clouds and ended the same. The days in between were the usual rainy gray. We stayed in an English home—a sanctuary of hearth and conversation, of family meals, of space to do our work, and to meet those sent for us to help. In between we gave our course, the LRT, in a hotel nearby to people known and some unknown. People have their past which replays in the present. People maintain memories of hurt which are no longer here. People have grievances which make them angry or sad. To be in the present requires the mind to let go. The refusal to let go is an unwillingness in all to be happy. Judgments are very stubborn to leave. "I would rather be right than be happy" is the theme of many minds. Can I admit I am wrong, languishing in a bad dream of memories, clinging to a position I defend, then dying in an accumulation of non-forgiveness? We associate intelligence with a good defense. Does happiness need a defense? It seems to be a state of mind free of defenses and attack, free of the victimhood of grievances. My week started with a clear firmament, went through the drizzling days of cloudy convolutions, then returned to the clarity of inner joy. A pax Britannia came over me as the green woods and cozy brick cottages whizzed by on the narrow county lanes to Heathrow. Certainly, I was experiencing Boundless Mercy.

106

Benevolent Forces

On the twentieth floor of the LaLit hotel in New Delhi we have an afternoon tea. The pigeons walk on the parapet outside our window and groom each other before the east view of the city. In the distance a building is being built. Men congregate on the top floor wearing yellow hard hats as they orchestrate the construction. A crane swivels around, high above, and hoists the heavy materials the men put together. Before this scene there is a train moving laterally across the vista. People walk across the platform casting long shadows in the late afternoon as the sun starts its evening descent. Another train comes as men run on the platform toward the open doors on either side of the coaches. Slowly the train moves forward after the people go into the empty holes on the sides of the cars. The platform is empty again. Only a few figures struggle in the bright light. I sip my beverage and munch the morsels of tiny cakes. The atmosphere of opulence is all around in the architecture and the care of the staff for the guests. Peace and quiet come to a crescendo; total appreciation envelopes me. What forces move us around this globe to be in high places that reveal the grace of God? Surely, they are benevolent to meet our needs with the elegance of beauty. Surely, they provide the means to rise above the lower levels of chaos. Surely, they bring with them the acknowledgment that Life is kind and good. I earn my gratitude every step of the way. And in these odes to the Divine Forces that shape the Cosmos, I recognize a Boundless Mercy.

107

In the Temple of Babaji

In the temple now. In the temple of Babaji, the maha avatar who is the guru of the gurus. Every year in the spring we go to India to honor the Divine Mother. The supreme cycle of life—adorations of the forces that keep all things safe in the universe. People come from around the world and converge on Herakhan, the home of this high master, to participate in this festival for nine days and nights. The hall begins to fill with many natives and their families along with Western devotees. Songs of devotion come in waves through the air, and a feeling of joy comes over me. The harmonium player sets the tone for the congregation to join in. Then the main song begins with the blast from the conch shell, a ringing of bells, and the deep banging of the drum. The Aarti is an offering of lights given in the form of a small platter of flames. A temple man weaves his way through the sitting crowd wafting the smoke of flames and the light over the heads of the people. The music builds in the energy of adoration, as the many faces take on a countenance of joy. I feel a deep delight to be amidst the celebration of devotion to the master within us. The Joy increases as the music envelopes the temple in a vibration of divine sights and sounds. I sing the notes of the Aarti that I remember and hum along with the sounds of sacred harmonies. Servants of the temple take around the plates of fruit to distribute to the people. The sweet taste of apple adds to the good feelings of communal happiness in this setting of Boundless Mercy.

108

An Ageless Yogi

An afternoon in Herakhan, after our bath, we await an honored guest. He is a yogi, ageless, nimble of body, not an ounce of fat or extra weight, well-practiced in the postures that keep him fit and clear of mind. All his movements are graceful and clear with specific functions to accomplish. He shows us the positions with the saintly grace of one who loves those whom he touches. We gather around his feet and listen to his true words. He speaks in his native tongue, and one among us translates. All health is in the right movements, the right relationship with the elements, and in a divine connection to our Source. The true yogi in his later years of age gives us his knowledge acquired from long periods of silence and practice. Practice is the important aspect of his attention. Without practice the knowledge is useless. So, we must be practicing what he tells us for the yoga to work. Walking the talk is the only way to be true to one's self. When the body is in good health, it is neutral, and it does not distract the mind with the forces of nature, with the morning and the evening, with the natural properties of the elements. Every year we come to meet this man of God, who always shows our group of friends the essence of yoga. We listen and follow along with his instructions, most of which anyone can do. We all keep up in the spirit of joyfulness. The yogi has a stick, and he hits each of us on the back as a blessing. It is a sacred affair to receive a strong love tap from the end of his staff. We are all blessed by the yogi of Boundless Mercy.

109

In Herakhan

It is a hot day here in Herakhan as the morning sun rises high in the sky achieving its full intensity. The haze has burned off the mountains. We sit in the chai shop overlooking the riverbed that weaves its way through this range of massive sentinels. Far across the way are the temples, nestled in the nook at the base of Mount Kailash. People cross from this side to that, appearing small along the pathways that meander through the billions of rocks. The water flows in channels across a vast horizontal expanse of boulders and rocks, the current gurgling its sound above the lowlands. A flock of goats crosses the river and stops in the water for a drink. I take a sip of tea as observations flow to me. Spring foliage on the tree in front are that early lime green with pods of seeds forming amidst the clusters of leaves. All this comes together forming a picture of pure tranquility. Two flies land on my book and persist in their presence. I shoo them away and they return. I shoo them again to see them return. On the third swat, they leave for good. In the flow of what is before me, India offers a closer look at nature and the forces of cosmic Life that permeate daily existence. Even the rocks in the riverbed become divine. The rickety chairs in the chai shop become thrones fit for a king. High and low cease to divide experience into the desirable or the undesirable. All things meld into the one great form of Boundless Mercy.

110

At the Close of the India Quest

Nine holy days of worship and celebration of the Divine Mother are coming to a close. We are in our room packing. All our Indian clothes and accoutrements go into the canvas bags while another cycle of the India Quest is about to complete its circle. We are replenished in our souls along with the other devotees of Sri Babaji. The rains came today as the atmosphere became cool and windy. The hot sun hides itself behind overcast skies and we go within the quiet space of all endings. I close the windows to keep the cool air from gathering gusts of firm breezes. Thunder bellows amidst the mountains. A deep base of rumbling notes reverberates into the distance. Most bags are packed by now that we have completed our yearly stay. The last holy fire in honor of the Divine Mother had been performed for the benefit of many, even for the human race in general. Thunder continues to rumble in the far-off Kumaon hills. Wheat fields ripen just below us, prompting the villagers to the harvest. The women use scythes to cut the stalks then bundle them in sheathes they carry on their heads toward the places of thrashing. We rest a while awaiting the electricity to come on again. The generator makes its loud cadence, its motor fired up to restore power to the entire ashram. Soon the lights come back on. We take our afternoon bath and put on fresh clothes in which to greet our group of students later at dusk. Now there is quiet time to relax and restore ourselves afresh. We appreciate the spaciousness of this restful time. The Peace of God blankets the land and covers our souls with Boundless Mercy.

111

Hospitality of the Highest

There is a place in the mountains where our friends welcome us. In Dehradun, their house, called Annapurna, sits on high ground overlooking the vast valley below. We come, after the India Quest at Herakhan is finished, for a respite. Hospitality abounds with the gentleness of refinement. Our days become divine in their leisure, enabling us to slow down and rest in the space of total relaxation. These few days are the springboard for our future actions, providing a calm of sanity to the work we do around the world. A common bond in Babaji, the sadguru of our mutual respect, brings us together in this intimate sharing of spiritual truths. Conversation is about meaningful subjects, broad-based and relevant to our lives and times. In the living room an exchange of human concerns, basic to life, takes place. The TV does not dominate nor drown out our own intelligence. We brought a friend this year to Dehradun, a woman we know from Lebanon, who was welcomed as family, just as we were welcomed many years ago. Indian guests are treated with the highest regards. Scarcely can we duplicate this hospitality in the West. We are too busy with our agendas and plans, incessantly busy with all kinds of "doings." Here it is a different vibration—one of spacious calm in which human relationships take the first place, high above the activity of worldly projections. Even to sit together in silence is a blessing. The beauty of the view off the elevated terrace brings the mind to silence. The sounds emanating from the neighborhood below bestow a blessing of Boundless Mercy.

112

Perfection is the Present

On the slopes of the mountain amidst the gardens of Annapurna we sit in leisure under the shade of a lawn umbrella. Protected from the direct rays of intense afternoon sun, an occasional breeze blows pleasantly against our cheeks, cooling us down in the flow of good conversation. The birds make their song and sounds in the background while fritillary butterflies flit across the grouping of potted plants, attracted to the bright colors of spring blooms. The sweet fragrance of an unknown source of flowering wafts in the atmosphere around us. I hear the buzz of a lone fly in my ear. It comes and goes. The wholeness of creation is always present. We sit in the midst of a moment of universal proportions, at the cosmic juncture of this time and space which continually extends itself outside the confines of time and space. Vast is this extension without boundaries. My mind is suspended for this moment of connection. What effects go forth from this to touch the very nature of human awareness? What strife is justified within the reality of God's peace and joy? How few connect with it. What end comes from all our doings here on planet Earth? Perfection is in the present without need of adjustments. We can walk the mountain roads rising from Dehradun and see the glory of a divine expansiveness. I am dwarfed by the scale of a range that spreads into the distance as my friends and I walk upward along the way to Missourie. After some distance covered, we stop at a chai shop and have a morning refreshment in the quiet of Boundless Mercy.

113

This Mission

The travels to Europe on this round are complete. A circle has been made, and we are in our sanctuary of home. The road is our "home" as well, yet nothing compares to the peace and joy of being in our own surroundings. From the second we enter the door, there is a different atmosphere, a more charged energy of holiness, a more focused arrangement of sacred space and objects. Babaji's presence is in full force emitting from His full-life portrait in the hall. We play the Aarti in the morning to honor Him and to lift our spirits into higher realms of awareness. Relaxed and at rest in God, our place in D.C. is the grounding rod of His teaching of Truth, Simplicity, Love, and Service in this part of the world. You sent us here to be our true Self in this mission to spread Your light to those we meet, to those who have influence over the state of affairs. We are here to receive a new Grace upon our land, a new vibration that can shift the energy of this new world to fulfill its destiny—one of real freedom in all realms of being, in all echelons of government, in all levels of society. This action begins with us in our own quest to follow higher laws consistent with the ways of the Cosmos. We dedicate our true will here to the attainment of Immortal Life, to banish the notion of "death" and "suffering" from our minds. In so doing would our time here in be useful to all our countrymen and women, to the people of this world who are looking for Boundless Mercy.

114

Deeply Seeing Beirut

Sitting on high ground well above the ancient city of Beirut, looking out from the balcony at the home of our friends. For five thousand years has this place of Mediterranean trade thrived. The Phoenicians went all over the sea in ships of commerce, forming one of the first written languages. Further refined by the Greeks, the Eastern Mediterranean cultures grew to build the basis of modern civilization. I observe into the distance of miles and miles an urban conglomerate. Billions of tons of concrete stretch out over the land in an endless sea of structures that form the city. How did it arise? How many hands worked in the heat of the sun to bring forth this megalopolis? And now, different factions in conflict. Why? One world, one people, yet to be realized as we war and dispute among ourselves. This construction of urban mass goes to what end? Ancient merchants traded their wares in all foreign ports of the vast sea. Commerce was paramount. Even now does it seem like a city of great trade, with ships being loaded and unloaded by great moving cranes on the docks at the water's edge. I look out over a vast cityscape of buildings large and small fathoming the energy needed to construct such a thing. In the quiet of my heart does all this seem superfluous. What is necessary is a meeting with truth, with simplicity, and with love in the heart of my soul. And let me not forget this most important Identity of Boundless Mercy.

115

The Continuity of Creation

Life, dearest Life, let me not utter an untruth. Let me not falter from those actions you would have me do in those most difficult moments when the way is unclear, and the conditions are grim. Let me receive the gloriousness of Creation into my heart and not judge the Cosmos based on my small corner in this world. You would have me rise into this glory that is mine as well, into the light of truth, into the beauty of simplicity, and into the all-pervasive grace of Love. Would I serve you in every second of my days? Would I feel Your Joy or wallow in the sorrow of my own making? Life, you are unending in the continuity of Creation, in the flow of rivers, in the expanse of the sky, in the relief of one breath. Why not myself—unending as well? Is there any part of me not of You? What is this thing we call "death," the ending of our physical form, the aging of this unit of measure to which we have attached? Let me not pledge my allegiance to death. Let me look death in the face and win my case for life in all conditions, in all situations, in all apparent challenges. Let my unending Self have dominion over my cells of Your good reason. Life of my Life, there is no death You have said. Make me aligned with only You. Make me certain that death is but a choice and I can choose Life over death, and Your immortality is mine as well. I am a piece of Your Cosmic reality, and in this realization would I not falter nor ask to end this demonstration of Your Boundless Mercy.

116

Prayer, The One Light

I write to Prayer, that form of speech which puts my mind to rest and lifts my awareness to the stars. What vastness are You, Prayer? Certainly, beyond my common words and thoughts You come to me in those quiet moments in the space between the ramblings of daily life. I take a "time out" from all of that, stop the game and huddle in the middle of my playing field. What next? I call to You, Prayer, to give directions to my soul in times when I have lost the way. Always do You guide, even in these times when silence and non-action are the words upon Your lips. I invoke You, Prayer, to be my muse in brighter moments when play is flowing toward our goal, toward the one homecoming of our joy into the parade that proceeds through the venues of my day. You sit atop the flowered float of reason with a scepter of majesty upon which sits the glowing orb of Truth, shining the ever-spreading rays of clarity. All this do I approach when I come to You, dear Prayer, to restore the important parts of my life's celebration. Help me achieve my goal of total remembrance of who I Am as God created me. In this recollection is my universe brought to harmony, my purpose made straight to the post of perfection, my destiny fulfilled in the book of Life. You are my one friend I would take everywhere I go, my ever-listening confidante who never tires to lend a listening ear, my director of deliverance from the tangled situations I have made. Open the gap for me to run through, Prayer, when all looks blocked and ruined. You are the one light that shines forth into my night with Your Boundless Mercy.

117

An Evening in Paris

Paris is a place of beauty attracting me to greater and more loving perfections. In the home of our friend, I take my evening time on the balcony overlooking the backyard quietude below and the wall of green foliage of the privacy screen of shrubs and trees. I have my warm beverage and the freedom to observe the dusk, when shadows are absent, yet night is not yet. The neighbors below complete their outside tete-a-tetes and begin to clear the tables of the remains of the meal. Now I am here alone, without the voices in French of others. In the distance there is a drone of traffic sounds, and overhead a plane is cutting its sound across the evening sky. Some children in the next building are still engaged in play. All sounds meld together in a song of twilight tranquility. A dog barks its common bark, a universal language for all to hear. My thoughts are slowing, and I observe the gratitude which fills the spaces between my thoughts. A profound stillness blankets every object at the end of my gaze; each thing a jewel in the reliquary of life possessing its unique properties and standing in true identity before God. The neighbors below return and make music in a language I do not understand, yet in their friendly soft tones I can feel a loving exchange between them. They light a cigarette. The flame flashes brightly in the darkening daylight, almost an explosion of yellow-orange brilliance in the murky grey-green dusk. All such beauty in Paris, the city of lovers, in this observation of Boundless Mercy.

118

A Garland of Living Blooms

I am at rest. Nothing on my mind before the day takes shape. We have taken our early walk along the river, down to the bridge just past the ballpark. It is a clear day with not a cloud in the sky—still cool in the air of late spring. Now I sit in our spacious apartment at rest pondering my next move while listening to the Aarti, the Sanskrit hymn we play to start our day. People come and go into my mind. Some have passed for good from this life. Some are still going strong in their own directions, most likely not to encounter them again except by memory or some Facebook post. It is good to observe the passing of things—the dance of existence constantly moving, constantly shifting focus, constantly in contact with the new. Now we are in Washington with new circles of encounters happening. We ask You, God, to arrange these fresh encounters on purpose, to exact the most life force in every exchange. At rest in this day, I await Your directions in all that I do or not do. I hear praises to You being sung in the most ancient of ways. In short, these writings are adorations too—the conversations we share in the quiet moments of my day, in the space between the activities of doing this or that. My mind is still, in the receiving mode of whatever Joy comes to me. I do not need a plan, knowing Yours will suffice. You string together the actions of my day in a garland of living blooms placed along the shoulders of my journey home to You. This time of listening is Your greatest gift to me. This time of looking inward is Your blessing of a vista divine. What can compare to these moments of Truth before the day runs forth? This is the gift of Your Boundless Mercy.

119

Be Glad for Your Day

The early day is best for attention to the Divine. We rise and bring order to our bedroom, my consort and I, taking joy in the simple act of making our bed. Then we put on our "walking clothes" and prepare ourselves for a saunter along the river. Out the door, remembering the keys, down the elevator to the lobby, morning greetings to the front desk attendant, we emerge into the atmosphere of the great outdoors. We are in the Navy Yards of southeast Washington D.C. just below Capitol Hill. What beautiful buildings of residence have been built in this area, and even a baseball stadium for the enjoyment of our national sport. Clear walkways and small parks fill the landscape as we walk down to the river's edge. A boardwalk goes in either direction. On this day, we head east toward the sunrise, reciting our holy mantras on our mala beads as we walk. This is the way to have a spiritual practice work your attention to the Divine in the actions of everyday life. Pray while you are walking, notice God in the trees and shrubs, flow with the sacred as you move by the meandering water of the Divine Mother. Be a person having a spiritual experience all the time. Notice beauty everywhere. Make every second a holy encounter—which it truly is. "Be glad for your day, Markus," I tell myself. "It is unique and will never come around again in this way." Each moment is a jewel in the treasure trove of Life unfolding. What people really want is something sacred in their daily quest to receive God's Boundless Mercy.

120

The Law of Love is Inviolate

In this day there is space to be grateful for everything. Some friends cancelled our meeting to go to the baseball game, for which I had already bought tickets. I was sad for a moment, then snapped out of it. When plans go awry, they were not meant to be. When life shifts things around, the shift is always for the greater good. Why not? What good is it to pine over meetings run amuck? I am the sovereign of how I respond to the shifts Life throws to me. Will I react with disappointment or rejoice in the possibilities of the new—of the present moment of Divine perfection? Lord, let my words be always directed by You. If You command a change, let me follow. If You command me to be steadfast, give me the strength to weather any storm or even the onslaught of an opposing fate. Let me stand with You, certain that Your direction brings me peace. If there are friends who place other priorities over the bond of true Love, help me to gracefully let them go to explore the ramifications of their own choices, their own destinies. Let me not cling to attachment. It is an impurity You would have me release. I move into the immortal blessings of this instant's perfection NOW. Why would I doubt this universal law? Why would I make my petty plans more important than the Cosmos unfolding? It unfolds for me! It moves in the way of Truth. The meetings that do not happen were not meant to happen. I am free of these lesser plans that I have made. I am liberated by a fraternity of immortal brothers whose words are truth and whose truths are spoken as law. The law of Love is inviolate, possessed of Boundless Mercy.

121

Morning Meditations in Washington

It is a Monday, and the sky is dappled with clusters of white clouds. We took our morning walk along the river's edge and recited our mantras in silence. The joggers and cyclists passed us by, listening to their iPods, intent on effort. We just walked in a leisurely fashion toward the huge bridge to the east. The sun was doing its hide and seek through the clouds. A woman stopped in front of us and took a picture of the sunrise on her iPhone, then proceeded to walk fast ahead of us. We sauntered slowly down the boardwalk, past the Navy Yards, scooting by the huge cannon on display in one of the yards. It was a graceful walk in the genre of outdoor forays into the expansive beauty of nature. The Anacostia River, about a quarter mile wide where we are, flows gently down to join the Potomac a few miles westward. Between the two rivers sits Washington in its regal glory. We live here now, just a few blocks from the capitol to the north, and a few blocks east of the baseball stadium, in a loft apartment that used to be a foundry. We are happy to have exposed brick walls and a super high ceiling with a feeling of expansiveness. We look out our tall windows onto a vibrant neighborhood of apartment buildings, shops, restaurants, and the like. On the third floor, we have a good view. Returning from our morning walk along the river, we take our showers, dress, and complete our meditations with some writing. My words flow from a contact with freedom from any pressure or any motives. In the relaxation of this morning would I allow the Holy Spirit to speak through me in lines of Boundless Mercy.

122

In the Scope of Holy Encounters

We go to the corner shop where they serve drinks to get a cup of coffee. There are TVs covering the walls and rock music playing. Baseball is blaring on a few of the screens. A cooking show has a man flipping an omelet. Another screen shows a congressional hearing with the attorney general. The waitress brings the coffee, which is cold. My wife complains. They take it back and we wait for a new pot to brew. In the afternoon, the place is completely empty. We are the only ones sitting at the high wooden tables. The baseball games play on without much notice. The waitress brings new cups with hot, not cold, coffee. I add my cream and take a few sips. The music is blaring but I don't make out the words. It is a bright building with a clearstory above with surrounding windows. The light pours into the space and brightens my day with the effulgence of pure Joy. Our neighborhood is blessed with the peace of affluence. Productive people want to be around other productive people, and the effect of this desire is a village of wellbeing. We came to D.C. to spread the Light of Truth, Simplicity, Love, and Service, and that we are doing in our own way by just being present—on our walks, in our early morning meditations, with the people we have met thus far, on our forays to the White House and the museums. All the best of our culture is at our fingertips. All this no bigger or more significant in the scope of holy encounters than the cup of coffee at our corner shop. All are immaculate expressions of Your Boundless Mercy.

123

The Circles of Somerset Speak

In my town, out and about, sitting at a Starbucks having a cup of coffee in a leisurely fashion. The music playing over the airways is pleasant. I ponder foreign lands while sitting in my Washington neighborhood. We go soon to the North—to Poland, Estonia, Denmark, and Sweden. Then we will converge on Glastonbury, the heart of planet Earth. Out of this Somerset energy of ancient Avalon, the Mother of all things spreads Her intricate designs among the fields of wheat and grains in crop circles of more and more beauty. The intelligence of this earth itself manifests these things. When will we listen to those angels of Truth and Beauty? Life immortal is their message. Harmony and perfect peace are their qualities. Listen! We have been deaf to Truth and blind to Beauty. How can we continue in greed and conflict in this world of man-made problems when these endanger our very existence? The circles of Somerset speak otherwise— intelligence is in harmony with the natural forces, and with the ideal forces of mathematical and geometrical order. There is no cause for anger, fear, and conflict. We all have what we need. What is the problem here? There is no problem in life we did not first manufacture ourselves. Look again, humanity. What is happening quietly in these southern English fields is a message of profound nature. There are forces higher than my own trying to lead us from insanity into the order of Boundless Mercy.

124

A Haven of Well-Seasoned Beauty

In Old Town Tallinn, Estonia, at a restaurant in an old house made of ancient bricks and stones, there is an atmosphere of medieval times as well. The timbers in the ceiling show a different mode of construction. Trees from five hundred years ago form the support members, thick and roughly hewn. Upbeat music plays on the speakers high on the walls. We order a salad and drink some sparkling water. It is a leisurely morning on our walk through the narrow cobblestone streets, stopping to rest and replenish in this haven of well-seasoned beauty. The waitress is young, thin, and elfish. What nature permeates this land of Estonia making the people effortlessly connected to a spiritual dimension of joy? I am in the momentum of this joy. I am the beneficiary of a different vibration. I am in the happiness that is unaffected by past or future. We enjoy our lunch of Estonian delicacies—simple vegetables prepared in a careful way: diced red cabbage, small florets of cauliflower, quinoa wrapped with a cabbage leaf. The dark bread rounds it out. I am relaxing with a cup of coffee at the end of our meal. English is spoken to the guests, even to those from other European countries. It seems that English is becoming the "world language." North on the Baltic, the summer months illuminate the sky with a clear azure blue, often cloudless and clear. We can be in the light of this enjoyment. Gratitude spreads through the streets of this Old Town. My heart picks up the vibration of appreciation. My heart goes forth to embrace the people of this holy land. I am in the flow of an action that shows me these aspects of Your Boundless Mercy.

125

To Observe the Expression of Life

Sitting now at a table in an elegant hotel near the front windows, observing the street scenes of people passing by. Sipping a small Jägermeister and relaxing after work. The late afternoon is overcast and cool. A woman alone sits outside smoking a cigarette and drinking a beer. Some tourists take photos near the sculpture of a man with a top hat. A handsome couple walks along with a child in between them. A taxi rolls over the cobblestones and makes a rumbling sound. In this late afternoon hour, the sun begins to break through the clouds, illuminating the bromeliads on the sill beside us. Blue sky peeks through the gray clouds. More tourists with cameras cluster around the bronze man, snapping photos and posing for momentoes. The smoking woman lights up another cigarette and takes another gulp of beer then scrolls down her mobile phone. The building across the street is painted pale green with white trim and houses Sotheby's and high-end shops. In between writing lines, I take another sip of Jägermeister and enjoy the deep sweetness of its unique flavor. There is an atmosphere of appreciation in this Estonian scene of leisure. What time is there in our day to observe the expression of Life before us? Too busy in new routines we miss out on the beauty of everything. How can a person slow down and give attention to this moment of Now? I am in this hotel listening to the pleasant music playing over the air waves and enjoying the time to write about what I see. There is beauty to behold and the richness of Life gives forth all the reasons to affirm the presence of Boundless Mercy.

126

Business at its Best

Stockholm on a quiet Saturday morning, sitting at Starbucks having our morning coffee. I relax into writing an ode. The streets are quiet and empty. We are the only ones sitting in this spacious interior. The white noise of the machinery hums in the background, competing with the music playing over the air waves. Our coffee is served in large ceramic mugs—not the usual paper cups. I enjoy the delicious dark brew as I jot down a few lines. Other customers saunter in. A couple orders at the counter then hug and kiss, one in his Hawaiian shirt, the other in her canary yellow blouse. Now others fill the space with activity. A man with a grey beard shares some Swedish conversation with a friend at the table next to us as they bite into their crusty bread sandwiches. My wife finishes her coffee and does not want any more. The lone server is now busy preparing the orders for a long line of people. This is a community of sorts—worldwide in its scope— where people gather to relax, drink a brew, check the internet, and get on about their business. We feel so free in this environment of global comradery. Business at its best is a place where people feel taken care of in connection with one another. It is not just about selling and buying, but more about connecting and relaxing, having your needs met. Here in the southern Stockholm neighborhood, the Starbucks is our place of convergence. We meet the people in the most basic way and have the space to be in grace. I observe the beauty of Life that reflects Your Boundless Mercy.

127

Sunday in Stockholm

Sunday in Stockholm, the sky is clear blue in the early morning. We meet our Swedish friend to collect our laundry and go for a coffee. She likes expresso. Such a small and concentrated shot of strong brew. We hang out for a long while in conversation before the other events of the day approach. On the street, still quiet with few pedestrians, we walk along the sidewalk observing the shop windows. Smart clothes in the various displays appeal to my fashion-conscious wife. It is a time to give thanks for all the providence of Life that takes us around the world to spread the good news: "God's peace and joy are mine." All situations lend their beauty to my days. We saunter along the Stockholm streets on this pleasant summer day, greeted by the happiness of appreciation. Returning to our apartment building, we key in the code to open the door and ascend the short steps to the elevator. We rise in the small chamber to the fourth floor. At the end of the hall I insert the key in the locked door and twist. The brightness of the apartment envelopes us, the dark hallway left behind. In the kitchen I open the balcony door allowing in the fresh Sunday air. We sit at the kitchen table and check our computers. All this is in a day of delight in the simplicity of movements that compose our visit to the North. In this bright summer, we are glad to be in the Swedish capital. For centuries, this town by the sea has been forming amidst the archipelago of islands of green. We enjoy it now, in the Sunday peace of Boundless Mercy.

128

A Symphony of Grace

Friday in Stockholm. It is free and clear, in the cool atmosphere, partly cloudy in the city south of old town. I am with my consort in a nail salon, waiting while a new manicure takes shape. The pretty woman behind the counter is from Vietnam, speaking a little broken English. The bell chimes in the distance, and a small fountain gurgles behind me on the window sill. The sun bursts out brightly as I view the fuchsia-colored orchids on the windowsill in the mirror. The cars whizz by and make a loud sound disrupting my listening to the gurgling fountain. A manicure takes some time, so I wait patiently for it to unfold. Women like to paint their bodies in various ways. Men seem to like it, as I do. The woman behind the table is focused on her work. She converses with my consort about coming to Sweden to marry a Finnish man. Seven years to learn Swedish, now she is conversant in this local tongue. By and by the job is done. We move on to the art supply store up the street and I select some materials for a small painting with the colors of the Swedish flag. The day is unfolding as it should and some other stops for various needs unfold in the afternoon. Eventually we end up at our local Starbucks for a cup of coffee. My consort reads in her book as I finish this ode. It is a leisurely atmosphere here in this place of community gathering. The sounds of business behind the counter, the clanking of coffee cups, the swishing sounds of the machines, all form a symphony of grace. I am relaxed in the flow of the day, here in Stockholm, the town of Your Boundless Mercy.

129

Goodbyes and Beginnings

Our last day in Stockholm is gray and rainy. It could be a doldrum kind of a day, but it is not. It could be a reason to be sad, but there is a gladness in me unaffected by the external situation. We stayed in this northern city for ten days and had some work with clients. We used our time wisely as the days passed by, and now we are on the eve of leaving Sweden, heading for Glastonbury. Our flight is early morning, and we arise even earlier to pack and get our transport to the air terminal. Our friend picks us up in her big car with plenty of space for luggage, and we head towards the motorway through city scenes and dimly lit tunnels that pass under the streets above. Soon we are out in greener places of town, zooming down the highway in conversation, recalling our glorious times together. We discuss the situation in Venezuela which has deteriorated into fear and chaos for many people. Our Swedish friend raised her family there and now she lives in this Nordic land away from the dramas of troubled politics. Yet concern lingers for family living back in the turmoil, amidst the uncertainty and danger. Rushing down the road, looking for our terminal, headed to green England. We unload our luggage onto the carts without any stress. In the moment we say our "goodbyes" to Sweden and Eva, which are not really endings but beginnings. Our time is complete for now in this Nordic land, in the cycle of Your Boundless Mercy.

130

These Ancient Grounds of the Grail

At the Chalice Well here in Glastonbury, we gather around the font of Your Living Water, one short of twenty. Among us is a Goddess of the plants, who knows the love of tinctures. She has distilled the nectar of the blue lotus for all of us to partake. The women receive another tincture as well, drops of the Divine Feminine; the men are given drops for the Divine Masculine. We go around the circle each receiving the appropriate drops. All are in a place of stillness and silence that pervades this place as we go deeper into the quest toward immortal life. I can feel the gratitude welling up in me, for this place and for the cycles of life which bring us around here again and again. I feel at home in these lands of Somerset each visit we make annually on our rounds about this Earth. The waters of the Michael line and the Maria line which circle the globe both converge in this garden. People come here to drink the holy nectars of Truth, to purify their minds and souls, to receive directions for the next phase of their life. Peace encircles this living spring of Truth. Joy is abounding in the plants and trees, in the stones and pathways which meander through the gardens divine. Energy pulses in our bodies and infuses our souls with gladness. There is a place in us where the stillness of God has its rest, and we connect to the truth of tranquility which is our natural state of being. Let all but this gently leave our minds, that we may claim our victory of peace. On these ancient Grounds of the Grail we sit down and remember You, Life of all Life, in these midsummer days of revelation. We breathe the glorious air of Boundless Mercy.

131

An Occasional Anchovy

Out on the town, we walk down the long boulevard from our venue to the corner Italian restaurant, anticipating satisfaction. Recommended by locals, the place is in a square building amidst a parking lot. As things go, often good food is not accompanied by any special ambiance. The inside is carpeted and full of white-tableclothed clusters of tables for four and for two. Half of them are full of customers. We are shown to a table in the middle toward the far end by the fake fireplace. Seated, the wine list and the menu are simple: one column for the food, two columns—red and white—for the wine. We choose our wine and food, a dry white, Caesar salad, linguine with nuts and spinach, and spiral pasta with broccoli. They come in stages, starting with a basket of bread and whipped butter. As usual, I cannot say no to bread. We sip our chardonnay and enjoy the bread. Soon the Caesars show up. The day has gone by quickly, which made me hungry. An occasional anchovy is good for the soul. There it is on top of the mound of romaine lettuce. A short time after, the pastas show up. We savor them and share a bit at the end. I take a few bites of my wife's linguine, then hand back the plate. My spiral pasta disappears into my unexpected appetite. We sip our wine and decline dessert. Awaiting the check, now it is time to appreciate the day and enjoy our night out in the atmosphere of Boundless Mercy.

132

The Sacredness of our Togetherness

In the north country in the early fall, the deciduous trees still have their leaves. No colorful hues have yet emerged, so we are still engulfed in green. At dusk, the sky is overcast, the ominous clouds stop short of a bright horizon—the blackish green. Silhouettes of the tree line sway against the vanishing brilliance of the day. A few cars drive by in the increasing dark. Now I can only see the red taillights brightly shooting across the murky darkness, disappearing into the distance. The crowd in the restaurant increases its volume. We order our food and wait. There was no linguine on tonight's menu. Something else struck our fancy. Maureen with us, we got to know the local color of her hometown. Events of childhood in a small town are similar to our own. The stories drift mostly toward the rebellious teenager era, just prior to moving away. The manicurist on the main street was a major hangout. What better place to plot some insurrections! All this, decades ago. Now, back in a time beyond recollections, in this present moment having a sip of chardonnay. The food arrives and our attention we give to the sacredness of our togetherness. Holy time is any time this sacred atmosphere is involved. The body of Christ is within us as we munch our meal and appreciate the return of innocence in this dinner of Boundless Mercy.

133

The Rainy Season

In Bali again. Every December sees our return to this magical land. This is the rainy season. In the still afternoon, I sit observing the droplets descend in their fall from the grassy overhang on the edge of a well-constructed slope of the roof. I hear the rain's regular occurrence most afternoons. Water, falling and flowing, soothes my mind and soaks the green land, filling the rice fields with pools of fertile reservoirs needed for bountiful growth. For the most part, green dominates the landscape with an occasional flash of magenta leaves springing up in corners of our villa's garden. Natural materials of stone and wood compose our villa. Marble covers the floor inside and the veranda. A table of teak wood rounds out the venue where I sit to jot down some words. Aspiring to beauty, which is also Truth, the twilight comes amorously amidst the rains, as everything slows down to greet the night. There is a vast space in which to relax and do nothing but appreciate this beauty. The sound of rain striking the roof and other surfaces fills the atmosphere with a staccato reverberation. A Balinese prayer is chanted far in the distance with its deep moans of elation. I anticipate our gathering at the dinner hour. The rains are waning away while the water permeates the landscape. In Bali again. The experience of rain indelibly touching my recollection in this island of God's Boundless Mercy.

134

These Gifts of Holy Abundance

The morning sun illuminates the ripples on the surface of the pool flowing out from the jets. The yellow ochre stucco shines bright as a backdrop for luscious green tongues of the lily's foliage. The constant shrill of cicadas is playing in the trees just outside our garden. I pull the long drapes on their tracks, opening the portal for immense light to enter our room. The refrigerator and air conditioning unit emit their white noise as I relax into a deep listening. Beyond the body's senses, what is there to see, hear, touch, taste, and smell? What is the fragrance of silence? What does a harmonic convergence of the heart look like? Can you touch the sweet smell of inner contentment? What is the taste of Love's holy morsels? All this nectar fills my cup to the brim of overflowing as my morning is spaciously receiving the congregation of sacred elements. Earth, air, fire, water, and space are given in this Balinese heaven. What is there to do but to receive these gifts of holy abundance and give them back in gratitude to my Creator? Love is Life and Life is Love. Can I appreciate each moment of Life with an ecstatic joy? The constant happiness of Creation is my inheritance to claim, as each instant is as potent for producing delight as all the rest. In this landscape of fertile providence there is an abundance of beauty to observe. Even the afternoon rains with strong downpours make my heart glad. The thunder rumbles loudly, shaking the atmosphere out of complacency. I count my blessings and give thanks for the flowering of Your Boundless Mercy.

135

A New Direction Unfolds

It is the last day of the year, number 365. Why do we measure time dividing it into endless increments? The cycles of the seasons are obvious enough to show us the natural order of things. It is winter now in Washington, and I need a coat to venture out on the streets. Today there is space to move and breathe in leisure. Our apartment is cozy, and we have the good grace of abundance in our life. All our electronic devices keep us connected to a broader world outside the confines of time or space. On this December 31st, let me dedicate my life from this moment on to greater and more loving perfections. This takes no time to manifest. Only a shift in my mind can open the floodgates of abundance. I invoke and dream AWAKE! In this new movement forward, all the minute things in my life are worthy of adoration: the brown oak tabletop, the chord that connects my laptop to the electrical supply, the blue bottles on the counter filled with fresh water. All these small things extend themselves into infinity, forming the ambiance of my world. On this last day of the year, a new direction unfolds revealing itself as I go. My job is to remain forever faithful in the presence of the unknown. My job is to stay in constant Joy in the face of conflict, undismayed because I am certain of Your Boundless Mercy,

136

On New Year's Eve

The afternoon is poised to receive our guests who come for a small repast. We are waiting for the new year to arrive as well. The young woman and her mom enter our place dressed in black winter woolens, looking remarkably alike, though separated by two decades in age. They come through the entry hall flanked by the goddesses, past the Quan Yin and the life-sized photo of Babaji. Stopping just outside the first bedroom door, we converge for a holiday hug. Surprised at the resemblance in features and appearance of youth, we make our greetings and shift to the dining area of our Washington loft. A chicken/corn soup was prepared and Vietnamese spring rolls alongside. Red wine in a glass served in tandem as well. The conversation filled us in with details of family history and dynamics—traits and tendencies. After the meal, we all went out to a movie. It was in Georgetown so there was a 20-minute drive in the car to the theatre which had a bar and leather-cushioned seats. The movie, about the finest hour of the *Washington Post*, the expose' on the Pentagon papers, revealed the lies told about the Vietnam War to the public. The truth being told, administrations exposed, our business in that place not just. How can we atone for a past of errors our ego wants to hide, except by Boundless Mercy!

137

What I Love About Morning

What I love about the morning, the day yet unformed, as it begins to rustle with coffee cups out of cupboards arising to meet my lips, is that the wondrous possibilities of miracles yet to happen spread their vistas before me. It is good to not quite know the dynamics of the day ahead. Certain enough is the distant swatch of morning sky in the bottom quadrant of the view out the window—a brilliant powder blue with some long strands of bleached pink clouds cutting diagonally across the short segment of horizon. The south side of a tall glass building reflects like a royal mirror at Versailles the drama of the morning sky, dividing with its ink black grid the scene of sunrise. The other buildings, still asleep and blanketed in the fuzzy shadows of grey, are only so slightly opening their eyes of vivid grids interlaced in the revelations of morning light. Pounding of the pile driver in the nearby construction site beats in the cadence of regular intervals, waking up the day like the abrupt shock of an alarm clock. I still sit in my pajamas, grateful to be free of nine-to-five demands, resting in quiet observation of my world unfolding before me. Every detail is a jewel in the treasure of this inevitable gulf of morning light increasing intensity as it adds to the emerging dawn of Your Boundless Mercy.

138

Anticipating a New Cycle

It is a wintry day here in Washington, with more snow to fall later in the evening. The white blanket covers the roof of shops across the street—a solid white rectangle stretching across the vista of the living room window like a ribbon atop the box of holiday rejoicing that came and went. Now in the aftermath of the New Year, I scan my day in silence, resting in this time of completed actions, anticipating a new cycle of events to unfold yet in this stillness of winter. I would love these times of external dormancy when introspection seems natural and the activities of the day are reduced to a few snowflakes floating across the close spaces between one season and another. In two weeks, we will fly to Florida and be in the warmth of southern climates. Yet now we wonder inside, and spend our quiet days on the couch, relaxing into a new cycle, a new season of travels. My wife reads the tabloids and fashion magazines, doing her research on the stars. I have my office on the kitchen table spreading my papers across the darkened oak, appreciating the warmth of our apartment in these frigid times of anticipation. This moment I observe the table-scape of things: my computer and devices, a stack of papers to tend to, a small pile of books, an antique glass vase with a bulbous bottom illuminating a rose glow, some pens nestled in a black woven sleeve, my wallet and watch awaiting my attendance. This scene of small things composes my New Year of Boundless Mercy.

139

A Walk to the Market

A walk to the supermarket was cold but cheery on this Sunday of cloudless skies. The crisp, frigid air filled my lungs with vigor and gladness to be alive. I entered the busy store and made my way to the soft drink aisle to fill my basket with seltzer water. Ten bottles later found me in the checkout line, awaiting my turn. A lady ahead of me had a basket full of sundry items which loaded into two full paper grocery bags. Heavy, I thought, how will she ever carry them? My checkout was simple after telling the checkout lady the seltzer was on sale, 5 bottles for $4.00. I saved 90 cents, liking a bargain, and not wasting a penny on the essentials. The lady smiled behind the counter as I tried to give her a tip, which she refused—against store policy. The two cloth grocery bags I brought along held five bottles each making a well-balanced carrier of our citrus-flavored water supply for the next couple days. Sidewalks of brick form the two-block route from our building to the Harris Teeter grocery store. It is a pleasant walk past apartment buildings well maintained, interesting first-floor shops, and the Department of Transportation—all new buildings or refurbished old ones. We live in a beautiful city in a neighborhood that is upscale. I am delighted our masters sent us here and we obeyed without a glitch. I am grateful for the help we received from our friends, graciously given with no expectations of return other than the instant gifts of God. My walk to the market revealed the Grace in my Life, heaven sent from the one decision to be in this Truth of God's perfection which pours into our Life of Boundless Mercy.

140

A Shangri-La of the Soul

Another year passed, and here we are again in Herakhan for the spring Navaratri. On the banks of the Ganga amidst the hazy mountains, we sit at the tea shop overlooking the spacious valley below. Old faces and new faces line the outdoor counter. I have a cappuccino and enjoy the stillness of the moment. The sun is burning off the mist, but the shade is still protecting us from the heat. I am listening to the conversation of others as the sound of the river below provides the backdrop for sacred music filling the air. Lofty stories are uplifting my soul and making me humble by just listening. Almost ready to leave this beautiful setting for another beautiful setting. We descend the 108 steps to the garden where spring blooms are lining the stone walkways. The atmosphere is perfectly clear with a gentle breeze rolling down the mountainside. In the distance the temple bells are ringing as the shoes of the master are carried down the 108 steps to the fire temple. Songs are played on the harmonium outside the temple and voices rise in unison to bless the procession. We honor our own sacred nature in paying homage to one who is certain of his own holy Self. The real vibration of this place is like a Shangri-La of the soul. I come to feel at home in my highest Joy. Fearlessness is placed in my consciousness in this home of Babaji, the immortal yogi-Christ of India. What is inside is outside. Do the trees fear? Does the river worry where it goes? Let me be as the mountain, content in its position in this universe of Boundless Mercy.

141

The Whole Thing Comes Together

In this garden of Your Love, the breeze goes through my hair and passes through the trees, moving their foliage in a gentle dance of morning movement. The sun over the mountain is rising higher in the sky but the shade of the trees is protecting us from its heat and strong rays. Stone pathways and beds of flowers and small trees spread before a place of sitting. We rest and observe the whole thing come together. The sound of the bells and the murmur of conversation surround us. In quiet do the elements combine in the miraculous, giving the grace of divine beauty every second of the day and night. People arrive to sit around the garden as the girls serving bring the tea in small cups. We receive our warm beverage and sip the sweet taste while welcoming old friends who have come from around the world. The man from the temple sits on a padded platform with a canopy overhead to shade him from the sun. Others come to pay him their respect. We observe the coming and going of the people into the tea garden. Soon, even we rise to cross the riverbed to the other side where the fire ceremony, then the group lunch will take place. The trail leads over stone walkways to the river's edge where the compacted earth shows itself meandering across the wide channel. Rivulets flow here and there with thick planks of wood acting as bridges. We cross the planks carefully as people move toward the area of the fire ceremony. We arrive there to take our place along the outer wall in the morning worship of Boundless Mercy.

142

Writing and Waiting

In another airport waiting for our flight with time on our hands. Already we have eaten. Nothing more to fill our time but wait. We check our texts and emails at the special counter for computers. Sondra looks at fashion sites while I write in my book of Boundless Mercy. There is a lull between flights, so the large hall is vacant now; still another hour before our flight begins to board. In the distance across the air strips, a green line of trees separate the ground from the skies. Rows of cumulus clouds stretch above the horizon and seem to float in suspended animation. An aircraft taxis across the runway to the takeoff area. One minute of speed-up and it rises above the ground in a matter of seconds. Small blue tractors pull wagons of luggage toward the terminal from the parked planes. The gangways to the planes jut out from the gates awaiting the arrivals, but the jets have not come. We are waiting as others begin to wait as well and the hall fills with anticipating travelers. The bright sun comes through the clouds and illuminates the gangways. An orange marker cone lays on its side in the parking area. Another yellow green one stands up straight, marking off the limits of the proper position for the plane. Conveyor belt vehicles are parked, awaiting the removal of luggage from the hold. I am writing and waiting. It is productive to notice things and make note of them. There is always something to observe, even when it looks like nothing much is happening. For we live in the throes of Boundless Mercy.

143

Enchanted in the Land of Enchantment

New Mexico is the "Land of Enchantment" where we are for a couple weeks. We stay with our friends who are generous hosts. They do their thing and we do ours then get together for dinner. It is a good relationship of mutual respect. We have our own guest suite in the far end of the house with our own veranda and door to the outside and fresh air in abundance. A hummingbird passes by, inspecting the flower beds. Small fruit trees populate the back yard. I am enjoying the gentle breeze sitting comfortably with my book of Boundless Mercy. The sounds of traffic on the highway are very distant, almost imperceptible. Birds cackle a bit in the trees. I hear a jet high in the sky. The clouds are dappled, spread across a broad blue backdrop. Morning light casts shadows at forty-five degrees making sharp shadows on the adobe walls of the house. There is a sense of calm. The space of the morning fills my heart with gladness. A perfect atmosphere comes into my lungs and cleanses me of all concerns. The hummingbird returns to feed on the red flowers, and then flies off rapidly like a dart into the distance. Voices are spoken from the fields outside the privacy walls. I cannot make out the words—probably gardeners of the adjacent property. I am enchanted in this space of beauty and total relaxation. There are elements of peace and quiet here amidst an expansive nature. I am grateful in this perfect setting to have the leisure to write. I sit observing what I see, inside and out, feeling the gentle breeze against my cheeks, making notes of Boundless Mercy.

144

On the Plaza

It is a bright day on the Plaza—late morning and the sun is nearly straight overhead. The open bench is unshaded so here I sit in the blinding light. It makes me sneeze a couple times. My consort is in the store shopping. There are many stores around the Plaza—all open for the tourists. An old man passes by with a dog on a leash. His spaniel on a retractable line sniffs along the ground, then barks at another dog a few yards away. A huge tour bus, out of scale, pulls up and stops at the red light with engine roaring and disturbing the peace. Soon the red turns to green and the bus passes on. Quiet is restored and the gentle breezes flow through the cottonwoods and meet my face. One side is warmed by the intense sun; the other is cooled by the blowing wind song. I squint at the page so bright and scribble a few more lines. Locals take up the shady benches whose conversations I can almost make out, but not quite. A car with all windows open, blasts its radio to the street. A tour bus with open windows comes around with a dozen passengers. I can hear the guide speaking to them over a microphone—they listen in a detached boredom. The sun is hot now. My consort comes out of the store empty handed. She comes across the street to express her disappointment, then soon is back to the next store in her search. A pigeon comes around, two feet away, stepping in an arch and on a mission of his own. Now it is time for us to walk back to the Eldorado Hotel to meet our ride. We must cover a half mile in twenty minutes. The traffic of cars and people continue around the Plaza. Now we arise to leave this scene to continue in the hands of Your Boundless Mercy.

145

A Hunch of Divine Inheritance

Finally, the work of the day is almost done, and I anticipate a success. Our writings will go out to the public through channels best suited. We are shifting our perspective on the matter, with an agent collaborating to have a publisher reaching the public eye. This is an action long awaited. We learned a lot in the interim of just exactly what goes into a book. I learned it, though I had no idea before. It is always good to be informed with the background of one's craft. Then you know what's involved in the creation of an art. So much goes into it; a dance of sorts which has its natural rhythms. One step at a time, a thing grows, without knowing quite how, into a palpable form that now can be reckoned with. Some may look and see. Others may not be interested. Some may be struck in the solar plexus of a divine connection. I cannot tell about the fate of my creations. Does God's concerns fall on the future? Most likely not. The cosmos unfolds in the present. The movement of Creation is always now. Now is the only time in which Life acts. No other instant is real; in fact, a book is done. Now is the time for it to go out into the greater consciousness of humanity. It will shift the minds of many. Even death may have something to learn—taking a sabbatical until further notice. Physical Immortality is yet a faith, a hunch of divine inheritance. Explorers of old went on a hunch toward the edge of the earth. There, they found no abyss, but rather the shores of Boundless Mercy.

146

Folding it All into the Fabric

In Pasadena, just north of Los Angeles, on a Monday morning after our seminar, having our Starbucks in the hotel café, I am writing. The large TV, divided into quadrants, hangs on the wall. It is presenting a game show of giveaways. It is silly and people are jumping for joy in the possibility of getting free stuff. Other commercials flash onto the screen. An ad for asbestos exposure tells people how to file a lawsuit for damages. A preview of *Survivor* shows people in the jungle preparing to crush their competition. All of a sudden, back to the game show. Now a white car with a buxom babe is on the screen. A couple is picking answers on a board for a while, then walk back dejected to their seats; apparently, they did not win. Now the scene shifts to another commercial about a drug you can take to prevent a heart attack. A middle-aged man, having dinner with his family, is escorted to an ambulance by paramedics. Apparently, he was not taking his drug. Back to the game show, a blonde woman in a black cowboy hat answers questions and wins an iPhone. She jumps and claps with more silliness. Now a commercial for people with sore feet and a machine in which to soak their tired toes. *The Young and the Restless* are now on the screen with snippets of drama flashing across the huge TV. Sondra is reading a book by OSHO— the guru who had a huge following. I am writing about what I notice and folding it all into the fabric of Boundless Mercy.

147

In Heaven Like the Day Before

The day has begun. We are having our morning coffee in the hotel lounge, sitting at the high table. A young lady works on her computer next to us and, after a few minutes, leaves with a colleague. The din of kitchen noise is all around us. Some of the guests sit in the upholstered couches under the TV having their conversations and coffee. My wife writes in her gratitude book for a while then gets up to go to the ladies' room. Now she is back to the writing. I take a sip of my brew and wait for the next line. Each day is like the one before, but not. There is a newness that has not yet been, and a memory that has passed downstream in life, never to return. And here and now I sit observing Bill Cosby goes to jail and Judge Cavanaugh gets grilled by the Democrats on his character. The public life of the exceptional is racked with conflict. But there is a reality free of conflict. Few want to go there and stay there. The day is new, resembling the one before. Once I choose peace, would peace not extend itself into the days ahead—into the moments ahead? Surely, I am in charge of where I will be in this decision. Heaven is here now when I stop projecting a hell. All my intentions are focused on this one decision. In the moment there is Peace. What would take me away from it? I let go of everything else. Here I am in Heaven, like the day before, drinking my cup of Starbucks in the Hilton Hotel of Pasadena surrounded by Boundless Mercy.

148

England's Lake District

It is fall, and the air is cool here in England. We are in the Lake District, where poets of older years sat under a firmament and penned their words that descended from on high. I am amidst their beauty, suspecting the similar air flowing in my lungs. Time goes by but beauty remains the same. Different people meander through the mists of dawn billowing up the slopes from water's edge. Our sojourn begins here in the little town of Windermere in an inn on the lake with the name the same. We had our breakfast in leisure, enjoying the scene of fall foliage through the floor-to-ceiling windows. Orange fire takes over the shrubs as they turn up their colors to give their last shout of joy before winter's dormant sleep. Just on the edge of a huge tradition yet to come to me--my observations given this boon of beauty's natural expression. All this coming together now from Wordsworth, Coleridge, and other weavers of words about to come to me still here, two centuries later. I am humbled. What could I add to the mountain of words that surround these lakes, so long the muse of hearts of men tuned to sing the praises of beauty? Mother Nature everywhere comes to a special wonder here in this Lake District which has drawn the arts to flower and spread its legends across the world. I see the bright morning light through the foliage of leaves encircling my view. A hawk dives and goes out of sight. Textured stucco of cream contrasts a backdrop to the magenta-turned ivy climbing up the English garden walls. Sitting now in my room completing the ode to You, Mother, who created this all. Let my pen follow my heart in this District of the Lakes, so much an agent of Boundless Mercy.

149

A Peace All the Same

A gray mist covers the morning scene with shadows upon more shadows. The trees remain asleep from the night. I am a bit gray myself in this observation of the stone-capped wall covered in the moss of incessant rains. A green lawn spreads forth from the house encircled by a dense foliage of evergreens. The music plays over the speakers in the dining room where we sit having our breakfast. The food is well prepared. I have a bowl of berries and granola for starter then eggs and smoked salmon. My wife eats an omelet. The only ones in the dining room, we have our meal in silence save for the music playing automatically over the speakers. The stillness increases in its intensity as peace envelops the scene. What is there to say? I listen to the silence and hear a bird cackling in the distance. A light sound of traffic comes through the trees from the town below. What poets sat here long ago and pondered the nature of their universe? In the midst of a natural drama, Wordsworth and Coleridge, friends, wrote of man's quest for the Self. Now I, in a similar place, with eyes fixed upon scenes just the same, though two hundred years of man's plight gone by—the massive killing wars behind us, but here, a peace all the same. What is time by a sleight of hand, a thin covering, when removed reveals the same gray patina of a cloudy, moist day? Nothing has changed, really, so why should I feel less than they, those greats of old who speak now as they did then, coming up from the lakes in mist of morning's inspiration. The bird crows again in the distance. The drone of traffic confirms a Boundless Mercy.

150

This Spacious Emptiness

In the Lake District of England, the hills are rolling up from the water's edge and small villages dot the shoreline. Windermere is where we are, in a hotel up from the town. Gardens and shrubs surround us, looking out into the yards while eating our breakfast. Another gray day with mists hanging in the fall atmosphere, leaves turning their fiery colors, and the morning waking from the quiet night. After our meal, we return to our room, back to the cozy warmth of an English hospitality. I sink into my world of stillness. In this place of emptiness, all is included as appreciation blankets the ten thousand things. Across an ocean in a different land, dawn is the same as night turns into day and the objects of beauty too numerous to name make a joyful noise unto the Lord. All the lands are enveloped in gentleness that surrounds me as well. Even words are cleansed and clarified by this spacious emptiness. I am open to receive the given. The beauty of this moment is upon me as I notice its finer nuances. A powder blue carpet spreads across the room, patterned with tri-colored arabesques. The day illuminates the scene with a positive glow. I catch some phrases as I observe other guests taking their bags to the car, loading the trunk, then driving off. In quiet Your Voice may speak to me of things unseen, amidst this beauty of the moment that spreads before me. Why not a beauty unfathomed by eyes or ears? Rather this quality of a listening mind to the order of things rushes into my awareness. I sit in silence and ponder the coming of Boundless Mercy.

151

Everywhere Beauty Abounds

The rhythm of this day begins with water. In this modern era of indoor plumbing, a brisk shower do I take with gratitude. Then clean clothes—another thing to appreciate—I put on in the bedroom, laid out in order by my wife. I give the next hour to God while sitting on the couch alongside my consort. Today, this looks like doing nothing. No practices compare to merely connecting to the sovereignty of my mind, observing my thoughts and the space between my thoughts. There is a quiet in the room which includes all sound. The brook outside the bedroom window falls, gurgling over the rocks, creating a steady song of glory. We walk down to the café for lunch, along a winding set of steps which snake through the hillside gardens following the stream on the left. The vegetation is lush and beautiful growing in tandem with the simple architecture. Everywhere beauty abounds. We sit in a small cabana with a grass roof in the middle of a pond. A school of striped fish hangs out in the shadows avoiding the intense sun. We sit and order our drinks and small lunch enjoying the gentle breeze coming up the sea and observing the bathers on the beach off in the distance. Our food arrives as we appreciate the service of the staff, all dressed in a light cadmium yellow uniform. With quiet and gracious actions, we are served our lunch by the young women who seem like handmaidens of the Divine Mother of Boundless Mercy.

152

A Late Thai Afternoon

A late afternoon in the café to relax and write. The sun is beginning its descent in the western sky amidst the soft gray clouds that fill the horizon. The girl in the yellow dress brings us water and takes our beverage order. Soon she shows up again smiling with a quiet contentment carrying our drinks, placing them gently in front of us. The foliage is all around, the turquoise pool spreads in front of the dining area, the cackling of birds is heard off in the distance, the voices of the staff murmur from out of the kitchen, a blue-shirted hotel worker carries a crate of utensils up the stairs. We have our late lunch then stand up to go back, descending the stairs to cross over to the other side of the pool. A natural spring contains a school of fish, striped, being fed by one of the guests. A feeding frenzy is active in the water as all the fish surge for every morsel. We cross over the small wood bridge to the stone walkway that surrounds the pool. Two large green ceramic elephants overlook the steps down to the lower pool. A few bathers relax in the water, gazing on the edge as they quietly observe the sea in the distance. We pass by and ascend the steps to the service road and head up the hill to the villas. The atmosphere is humid as usual in this Thai environment. Going up the road amidst the lush foliage we come to the path to our room. We turn right and the trail takes us slightly back down the hill, past the stream and the waterfall cascading pool to pool in Boundless Mercy.

153

In Conversation with the Divine Mother

Dear Divine Mother, I am infinitely blessed by Your Boundless Mercy, especially here at Besakih Temple, Bali. You have drawn holy families here for over a thousand years, and You draw us here as well, every year with our participants of the Bali Quest. This year we especially dedicate our meeting with You and include our nation, the USA, that You may enter the hearts and minds of those important people who can make a difference with You. Open them up and connect us with them in miraculous ways. We are here to serve You and Your people, without borders. We are here at Besakih to bring back Your Energy to the White House and to give Your Energy to those who have taken the vow of immortality at Your Crown of Glory. Help me to have a perfect diamond body that can serve Your mission into perpetuity. I am ready to receive Your boon of physical immortality for the purpose of divine service. Give me the directions You want for me and I will follow them. I request to see, feel, and realize some healthy shifts with my body. Let this day and every day be an expression of Pure Joy! Let me be aligned with perfect happiness and not allow anything external to affect this alignment. May all human beings be freed from painful karma and all thoughts of cause and effect that may bring suffering. May mercy rest upon the whole human race. Let forgiveness rest upon all things through me in the Christ. I dedicate this day to being my true Self in Him Who is Your Son. Please increase my Power of Love, Safety, and Certainty in Boundless Mercy.

154

A Statement of a Lofty Truth

I would *look upon the glorious reflection of God's Love, which shines in everything. I live and move in Love alone; I am not separate from Your eternal Life. There is no death, for death is not Your Will. I abide where You have placed me, in the Life I share with You and all living things, to be like You and part of You forever. I accept Your thoughts as mine. Your will is one with mine eternally.* (Lesson #163 in ACIM) You give me the supreme energy of Pure Joy to fill myself and give. The more I give away, the more I receive. It is my "para shakti," my source of true power. Love is the only power beyond our understanding, yet it is within us to use and to share so as to increase our own aliveness. Jesus says, "There is no death. The Son of God is free." (Lesson #163 in ACIM) This is a statement of a lofty truth, yet we must rise to meet it—to apply it in our life—which means to let go of all that is not true in us. All limitations are false. All sickness is a defense against the truth. All anger is a detour into "victim consciousness." All grievances are an attack on God's plan for salvation. Miracles can save us from all these errors in our mind, yet we need the willingness and love for correction. The miracle is a gentle correction introduced by the Master into our mind to give as God's Thoughts. All things come to me to make the decision for Heaven, once and for all. Who can make this decision and "never go back to hell"? That person has transcended thought and is with the stillness of the peace of Boundless Mercy.

155

Your Other Name is Life

O, Death, you are the giver of release, the ender of cycles, the emissary of life eternal, a servant of divine blessings to those in need of ultimate transformation. You are the fire out of which my new phoenix arises and resurrects myself in a new birth of freedom. I hold hands with you in facing the illusions in my life. You wipe the slate clean and bring the emptiness of silence, the space of void, the awareness of Love's certainty. The ultimate forgiveness and correction of all my mistakes, you are the grand master of total atonement. Call you Love in your mission to liberate souls from all suffering. Let me meet you now and live eternally, having passed through your doorway to the Light. There is no fear in me now, no pain to go through still, no business to complete. My work is done, my karma at an end, and only Immortal Life facing me ahead. Hasten my steps, oh Lord called Death. Your other name is Life, your other name is Shiva, the eternal slayer of illusions. Let me face you. Let me face my Self. Let me release all feelings of despair. Let not pain be in my body at all. Take from me this burden of struggle, this weight of tasks unfinished. I am the servant of the real face of you—Immortal Life of Joy. Take from me all sorrow and burn it in the fires of transmutation. Heal my body of death, of all that is not perfectly functioning. I call upon you, the real Lord of Life, to end all that is not Joy and perfect happiness in me. There are no more thoughts of pain and strife, struggle and defeat, lack and the scarce morsels of hunger. I am filled with your Light of Truth, your eternity of Boundless Mercy.

156

This Deathless Now

I die but I do not die. What "death" is this? The death that ends all death is the door to Immortal Life. The death of the thought that death is inevitable is the awakening in the mind to Life without end. This is the death which is the last, the one stop into heaven's pastures and gardens of fulfillment. I am in the stillness of the Peace of God where all things shine on in perpetual perfection. Each loving parcel of composition sits palpably in the Grace of existence before me, one object no more or less sacred than another. The table, like an altar to truth, holding what it will, each object on it a holy testimony of itself. I look at a thing and marvel at its beauty. It lives in the present without end, no past, only present happiness filling its neutral body. A ceramic cup, yet a grail of immortal Life. A chord supplying the computer with power but a lifeline into the future. What could I neglect in this collection of hallowed things? All pass into this deathless now. All sit in the remarkable veneration of common existence. The wood board on the counter is for cutting vegetables with the sharp German knives. The kitchen counter is granite, cold but durable for all time. I feel and observe what is here and appreciate it is good. All objects have their sovereignty—each sings of its own presence in creation. All are one in truth and contribute to our immortal state of being. The Now is always here in Boundless Mercy.

157

No Other Direction but Home

Resplendent peace surrounds me in Herakhan. This center of my soul, this center of the universe, the seat of Love in my heart would I take wherever I go. No place is void of Your effulgent light of eternal Joy. Swa ha! Let me pitch all my sorrows into the fire of Your ever-burning transformation and come away with the infinite Grace of God which surrounds me. Anger is all gone. I have done my work and taken the worst parts of me and laid them at the feet of my Masters. I breathe in the sweet air and smell a flowered fragrance of Your ever-present care spreading around me. The wellness of my Being abounds without limits. I can send myself to new worlds of Your Love and see the pure possibilities of my life. Let me flow into these new spaces of eternal delight and remain in Your Pure Joy which is mine as well. Let me forget all those distractions which bind me to the shadows of my past. Over those days gone by do I let forgiveness rest. Connect me with all whom I encounter in my day with a deep heart that sees into theirs. May I look into their eyes as though they are my own. Let me be You for a day, dear Holy One who is the light in my Life, and give Your Love through my eyes, my mouth, my hands, and my soul itself. My feet can take me where You want me to go. I have no other direction but home to Your Will that is done in me as in heaven. Allow me to speak the words You would speak and do the things You would do. All this would I realize by Your Grace, making my Life into a sacred song of Your Will, in the symphony of Boundless Mercy.

158

In the Core of Myself

In the temple with the drum and singing voices of the Sanskrit chants so strong, I listen in the core of myself. The boom of the drum affects me. I am moved by the deep vibration sounding in a regular cadence. Rising to a Joy within that is still, free of the external effects of ups and downs of worldly dramas. Now there is silence in the aftermath of songs. Mantras are recited and bells are rung over the Divine Mother's book. Again, the pulsing sound of ringing bells enters my heart with its cleansing nature. I smell the cow dung wafting off the field on the wave of a breeze blowing through the window. The people gather in a huge huddle to perform the puja to Babaji's padukas. Gradually the crowd disperses after the adorations have been made. Now the people prepare to read the 700 names of the Divine Mother in more honoring of Divine forces of Life. The many lines are recited in the atmosphere of receptivity. I listen and take in the blessings, going into an altered state of a trance. I almost pass out. My mind goes blank, yet I am here and now, aware of my body. For a spell I go out of consciousness of the senses completely, suspended in a state of being pure and serene beyond the consciousness of day-to-day life. This lasts for the duration of the reading of the names and comes to an end in the silence of the temple. My joints feel cleansed and fed when I come out of this samadhi as though the divine nectar of Truth has given them necessary lubrication. I am in the flow of this Divine blessing as my consort and I arise to walk down the 108 steps to Your river of Boundless Mercy.

159

The Energy of Sacred Infinity

Time in India takes my soul back to its origins. What else but the Mother of all religions could do this? Before humankind thought of its Source, India was waiting for this great awakening. Here I am now on her soil, in the Himalayan foothills at Herakhan in the Temple of Your Love. The chants of the Mother are being sung. Children run hither and tither joyously shouting. The deep drumbeats vibrate down into my chest as I am swept into the holy vibration of the chanting. A high-pitched bell is ringing as an ant walks across this page. Some of the people stand and sway with the rhythm of the music. Many others come and go to watch the main ceremony to the Divine Mother in the inner shrine. I sit on the outer perimeter watching this kaleidoscope of activity. Holy actions continue when the ceremony of worship is completed—a new focus shifts to the sacred book of verses to the Divine Mother. The song of the Goddess is sung as the bells are rung loudly and the drum is struck again. People listen to the ancient mantras recited and spin around three times. Now there is a lull. My wife comes in to rejoin me telling of some bad news from a friend whose brother committed suicide. Everyone is milling about in preparation for the 700 Divine Mother names to be read. Life goes on in the midst of death; Joy comes forth in the middle of sorrow. The Mother of the Universe stretches out beyond our thought, past the edges of a trillion universes. I am in India for a spell, engulfed in the energy of sacred infinity. Things come and go; people come and go; incidents of anger come and go, but You remain stalwart in Boundless Mercy.

160

The Harmony of Holiness

Afternoon has come. The sun has passed over its midpoint beyond the other side of our veranda which is now engulfed in shade. I sit at rest, looking out into the distance on the mountainside illuminated by the intensity of the passing sun. The line of the crest of the peaks meets the azure sky, forming a spectacular horizon. What stillness is this in all its massive movements of nature? The trees sway in the breeze, or the solar trajectory passes before me, almost imperceptible in its slowness. Shadows are beginning to lengthen. I am content to meld my mood with the peace of this mid-afternoon vision. One could be anywhere in a state of quiet observation and see the glory of creation in any scene, any subject, any situation. Yet in Herakhan, the space between the Divine and the mundane is diminished to zero, and here I am within the bliss of stillness. How can I maintain this state of being in the harmony of holiness which comes about when the mind is quiet? All things arise into my awareness of calm when I am disengaged from the world of thought and motives. Time extends itself into infinity with no past and no future. The things I see take on a beauty that is intrinsic, emanating out of the core of their being. Colors are brilliant, textures are tactile, sounds are sonorous in a harmony beyond words, smells are sweet in their holy fragrance. All the world around me comes in its appeal to be released into the wholeness of creation. Only in my mind is the shift needed, in my relinquishment of false judgments formed in my ignorance of the Truth. Peace and Joy abound in the reality of Your Love which shines on everything in this afternoon of Boundless Mercy.

161

India Within Me

In the Indian home there is leisure. All the modern accoutrements are there, but the TV is often off. We gather around lively conversation or classical Indian music playing in its calm grandeur, or simple sitting together having a beverage and snack, checking our mobile devices. There is no plan or agenda. Whatever unfolds is in the perfection of togetherness. Tonight, we all have a whiskey and cheese and crackers with hummus dip. The sitar and tabla are playing over the speakers by master musicians. The news is over, and we relax in the sanity of Divine Joy from the music filling us with the sacred sounds of an ancient tradition. Each note is so precise in its tone and duration, rising and falling in a cascade of musical ecstasy. Nowhere else but India could these sounds come forth. Musician saints carry the genius of holy compositions from generation to generation, passing on the tune and the player's prowess from teacher to student—from saint to mendicant—over the centuries gone by and into the infinite future. We are the beneficiaries of this great flow of living music in this moment of receiving in this friendly Indian home. At the feet of the sacred essence so prevalent in this part of the world, we are drawn again and again toward our return. Yet do we ever leave this reception of true beauty in the elevated heights of this Indian culture? Once touched in the soul by its sacred essence, then do I take beloved India with me wherever I go. There is no place higher when this contact with the Divine is made—no place that does not rise to meet India within me in her Boundless Mercy.

162

A Week in Amsterdam

Landed in Amsterdam, and with grace of good care we were met by Monique. We rolled our carts to the taxi area just outside the terminal and spotted a car big enough for all our luggage and three of us. It was a unique car—a Tesla with winged doors that open upward to the heavens. All our bags fit in the back, so I was happy with the ease and so was the driver. We traveled across the green fields toward town on the four-laned highway, catching up on our news. Soon in the midst of the city, crossing canals, observing the love of brickwork in the architecture, and appreciating our time here in Amsterdam, a whole week to be spent seeing clients and giving a lecture, we arrived at our Hotel de Hallen, next to an old market now modernized. Checked in, we strolled down the promenade to our flat, #9, up one flight of stairs. A spacious place on two levels, bed and bath upstairs, we are well situated for one week. What could be better? All our needs are met with an extra attention to spaciousness and good surrounds. A skylight makes the place bright. The wide-plank wood floor of white oak melds well with the view of brick walls just outside our window in the common areas of the promenade. Shops just outside our door give an air of human activity. Lively, yet also quiet, this Dutch scene is inviting us to great levels of Joy. I have a cup of coffee while the ladies go fix their nails. There is no pressure to be anywhere. This old town of commerce has been active for centuries. I am glad in this place of Amsterdam, where You place us within Your Boundless Mercy.

163

Embraced in Tallinn Town

Tallinn on the Baltic is one of my loves. We stay on the central square in an apartment facing the large public space, open and filled with people all through the day and night. The revelers never sleep. The joys of celebration rise up in that atmosphere, pouring in through our open window. We take this Joy into ourselves and feel uplifted during this stay in the ancient city. Characters in medieval costumes serve in the restaurants, giving an air of authenticity to the old buildings and environments. The food from days gone by seem unusual to our tastes, yet full and pleasant to satisfy our curious appetite. Wild boar, bear, deer, pheasant—all meats from the wild. We choose something less exotic—a mushroom soup that is the best we have ever had, and a honey beer in a tall ceramic mug with a natural grain bread topped with a swatch of cream cheese. We sit outside on the wooden chairs at the rough-hewn tables of thick, wooden planks. All has an air of medieval charm, but we know it is staged as an act for the tourists. The cruise ships dock daily nearby in the Tallinn port, emptying out their thousands of adventurers from foreign lands. Amidst this onslaught of sightseers, we weave our way through the streets of Old Town to an art supply store where paints and a canvas are to be had. I make my purchase and we head back to our apartment on the square. The apartment house has an elevator which is rare in this town of five-century-old buildings. All is provided in this Tallinn town of your Grace of Boundless Mercy.

164

Wherever I Am

Back in Washington for a while, I am at my table, wide, oak top of dark-stained wood amidst the great room that serves a dual function of living room and kitchen. The tall windows on two sides usher in a bright, late-morning light. The brick corner is a backdrop for the bronze Indian god, lit from below on his pedestal, a torso of Divine proportions. The gentle din of traffic sounds in the distance, as the whir of the washing machine faintly meanders into the definite sonata of my day. I have checked my emails and eaten my late morning brunch, the tasks of my day in full swing. Some are requiring more attention, yet I make a space to appreciate Your Boundless Mercy. It is always here and now—wherever I am, never fading into a half-present blessing contingent upon conditions of favor. Your Peace is always here, even amidst the small battles of warring thoughts and factions that pass in front of my field of daily attentions. Someone here in a crisis, another person there totally confused, a student who wants to get closer, and one who wants to move away from the fire of inner transformation. I give these conflicts over to You, Great Mother of Mercy. I cannot know the full extent of Your Love which would nullify all that seems to persist out of sync. You are the Great Harmonizer since time and space began. You are the Great Manifester of Light out of the endless Void of the Dark. Let me cling to this awareness of You in my times of doubt. Let me use Your clarity to dissolve at Home all these possible catastrophes that only seem to deny Your Boundless Mercy.

165

The Action of Grace

Can I remember You in the Present where You abide unchanged from the instant of Your beginning so long ago? It is not "then" which I would recall, but NOW in all its present Glory. I'm in an empty space of mental silence. Why put anything within this boundless reservoir that contains Your all? I have emptied it with diligent relinquishments. All attachments are released and what remains are only chords of Love which delineate the necessary ties to Immortal Life. Mother increase the efficacy of my forgiveness; make it complete. Let no one be cast out of its ever-inclusive beneficence. Make my body into a tool of Your Love. Help me to maintain its good working order and use it in Your plan to build a Heaven on this Earth. Keep my Life simple so I can serve better Your Will of perfect happiness. Keep my fires burning in the heart of my desire to be my True Self. Keep the flow of work coming to me for which I dedicate and devote my days. Make my reason to be Pure Joy. Envelope it like a sweet scent of Turkish rose perfume around all the actions of my days. Get me out of the way and waft this fragrance of divine fulfillment toward the play book You wrote out for me. I trust You to fill in the blank spaces of my uncertainty with the action of grace. I do not know the way to You, but You are wholly certain. Guide me along to remember You in this Presence where all decisions have been made to receive Your Boundless Mercy.

166

This Scene of Greater Gratitude

Back in our home we are relaxed in the mood of deep ease. The space to be present is a passion, and we are happy to be alive. Is it possible to be free of all problems? The wise are connected to a Force that is rising to Heaven at once. All things are engulfed in this vortex of well-being. Alone am I amid this plethora of life's common accoutrements. At the table do I sit writing Your graces of boundless mercy. Objects hither adorn Your divine providence: my beloved Mac, documents to be filed in financial folders, magenta glass flower vase with its bulbous base, a glasses case, iPhone plugged into the side of Mac for recharging, Mexican ceramic coffee cup half full with morning brew, a pile of pounds from our recent trip to England, passports awaiting our next tour of duty, spiral-bound notebook with essential info from recent encounters. All things together make up this scene of greater gratitude. I am listening, ever listening to the sounds of silence around me as each sacred thing emits a vibration I hear in the inner core of attention. I need nothing more in this day of delight to feel the holy abundance of all these things which bring me their Joy. Basking in the ordinary scent of everyday life, I find so much to appreciate. I touch the edge of heaven in these things of real presence. Now is the advent of all You promise me in this objectified compendium of Boundless Mercy.

167

Serenity of Sundown

It is a bright afternoon, late in the day when the sun has passed over the buildings and shines backward from the western horizon a crisp orange light. Things are warmed by this effulgence. Even the inside of me feels this fiery glow of color on the facades of my soul. The bricks of the structures down the street heat up and emit a maroon brilliance. The shadows of this illuminated scene have a sharpness of edges which contain the cooler tones of bluish gray. The distant sky in the east is still azure mixed with a tinge of violet white. God paints this picture of twilight serenity even in the bustle of the city. I observe from my window high above the scope of urban life a true account of what I see in this glory of creation spread before me. Always is there something to inspire and uplift. Never is there cause for anything but pure Joy, even in the midst of difficulties. I rest in this serenity of sundown to greet the night which is equally at peace. I surrender my senses to a different perception, one of beauty and grace that enlivens my awareness to include the colorful heat of Indian summer and the glowing warmth of a light cast backwards from the setting sun. I am in the huge gratitude of this very moment of Your Love. It spreads into my space through the windows of my holy observations, warming my inner sanctum with Boundless Mercy.

168

Great Spirit of Immortal Time

We changed the clocks today as the whole nation pushed back time to the standard version. One hour we lived again as though those minutes transpired could give us another chance to get things neat and tidy, and we could gain some new advantage in our brightest expectations. The sun rose as it always did, yet one hour earlier. Now it will set an hour sooner still, depriving us of daylight at dusk by sixty minutes. But God does not lose or gain, and the cycles of the Great Sun revolve the same for billions of years past and billions of years to come. Oh, that You would bless our home indeed, Great Spirit of Immortal Time. No beginnings and no endings taunt my mind with limitation. You are the massive movement of everything in the cosmic matrix of the all-pervasive Presence. What little shifts and tweaks of time could play any role in the universal Life of Your Will? The morning rays of Your Love still rise over the distant treetops and roof tops and horizon tops to engulf my soul. Everyone is warmed equally by Your effulgence of brilliant morning light— that light we try so hard to save, or to love, or to manage in our long string of never-ending days. I sit poised to anticipate this outpouring of illumination. What scenes will be revealed today one hour earlier? Will my world darken sooner from this shift of the clocks backward? Who decides these global manipulations of time? This interval of increase, either way, brings only more of Boundless Mercy.

169

Our Best and Brightest Self

Around the world we go in a circumambulation. These cycles become so essential as we rejuvenate ourselves and charge up our internal batteries of pure joy. Now we are in Kamalaya on the island of Koh Samui, resting and relaxing in this Thai atmosphere by the sea, soaking up the gentle ocean breezes in the warm shade of the Amrita Café. We have our lunch in leisure and scribe a few lines in our books. The staff is dressed in Naples yellow uniforms with the countenances of happy natures. They scurry here and there, tending to the guests. We sit in stillness appreciating the blessings of our good providence, looking over the gardens toward the fishponds teeming with a school of striped swimmers congregating in the shaded corner. A couple with German accents speaks lowly in an intimate setting at the table next to us. They discuss the dynamics of their day and the activities they plan for good health. At a wellness spa people come to detox and disengage. Easy here to relax, the spaciousness of Kamalaya is conducive to better living. We immerse ourselves in this flow of divine leisure, slowing down our thoughts, watching the movements of peaceful actions spread out before us. The huge granite boulders flank the dining pavilions. Are we as stalwart in our strength just to be? Life is an opportunity to show up in our best and brightest Self with the certainty of rock in Your endless and Boundless Mercy.

170

Now or Not at All

There is no vengeance in the Mind of God, no loss but only certain gain in the Life Force of Pure Joy. All my mistakes, large and small, are forgiven. What is this ascent into the full acceptance of my innocence? Why would I linger any longer in feelings of guilt or remorse of things I did wrong or things I failed to do in this great dance of Cosmic proportions? Great Spirit of this Universe, please accept my gratitude for my Life. Let me come forth in my full power to co-create with Your worlds of blessings, domains of Pure Joy, realms of resplendent beauty. I am here in your paradise. Why would I pine for something greater? Nirvana is now or not at all. My awareness of Your higher truths is only accessible in these very moments of Your timelessness. The breeze blows in from the sea, the morning mists roll down the slopes of the mountain, the melodious notes from the reed flute waft across this atmosphere of peaceful providence. We are at rest in Kamalaya among the lotus ponds and gardens of earthly delights. How could a thought of fear or duress enter this mind of Your Love which bestows only the possibilities of rich rejoicing. We feel the grace of all that is given. We play in the palatial settings of spiritual kings and queens. The royal road to our true Self is made so clear and straight, not any difficulty to navigate its narrowness. Let my mind be still and accept Your Glory which is my own. Where would You lead me but here in this victorious setting of certain Boundless Mercy.

171

This Harmonious Awakening

The morning wakes up to a set of distinctive sounds: the gushing song of the brook meandering around the large granite boulders, the early diners who take their places in the breakfast hall, the clanking of dishes in the background of the kitchen, the low murmurs of tete-a-tete conversation between guests, the flip-flop of the girl's steps across the terrazzo floor. I take it all in and relax, giving this observation my full attention. They bring us coffee—one black and the other with a small beaker of frothy milk. I have a cheese omelet with a few diced tidbits of veggies on the side. The visuals are awakening too: high above on the slopes up from the sea, I view an ocean coming alive in its soft azure blue, reflecting the rows of clouds which hover over the mountains in the distance. The palm bursts of the trees are like exploding tassels of yellow green shooting up into the center of my soothing vista of a tropical paradise. The sun coming up behind me illuminates the scene as the dawn draws everything it touches into this harmonious awakening. Let this be as well my resplendent escape from reticence—eyes open wide now in the coming of day, the slumber of my faculties done. Awake! This is the only real commandment of a Loving God. The dawn of my soul passes into this day, and the senses of my body align in consistent cooperation with the bounteous beauty spread out before me. I connect my insides with my outsides so there is no difference to behold in the Pure Joy of one melding with the Pure Joy of another. This Thailand garden of earthly delight confirms before me Your Boundless Mercy.

172

The Lotus of Our Soul

In our spacious villa here at Kamalaya we have ample room to spread our presence into the various levels of our little house of wonder. The cream-colored marble forms the floor of our living room, the sofa bends into the main corner and stretches long and wide—a comfortable haven for lounging and resting, reading, and checking our computers. There is a desk in the corner where I set up "shop." A respite includes connection to the outside world as communications never cease. There is a counter and bar top for beverages, fruits, ice bucket, and cutting board. Down a few steps to the lower level floored in wood, our king-sized bed is most comfortable. A finely constructed clothes closet made from teak wood fills one corner; a shorter version is adjacent to the bathroom door. A view of the sea through the trees and a vista of vegetation with the brook running through boulders below is seen from all points in our place. The bathroom is semi-outdoors. A curved brick wall forms the back of the structure with bricks carefully laid around a ten-foot-tall boulder covered in sea green lichen. A tree grows up alongside the boulder. Nature has a presence here, as though architecture is secondary and must meld into the setting and allow nature to take the first place. We are simply held in the arms of the Divine Mother with Her manifestations of divine things, holy elements that fill our awareness with gladness and spread before us gentle scenes of beauty unsurpassed. Kamalaya is the lotus of our soul, and we are awakened by its spreading petals of grace in very particular forms coming out from the central core of its flower, one of Boundless Mercy.

173

Perfect Tranquility

Closer to the sea now, just up from the grassy knoll and the pond of lilies, we can see the beach and hear the gentle lapping waves roll up the shore. Bathers sit under beach umbrellas sipping their afternoon beverages. A young woman in a bikini adjusts her top then sits back down in the shade. Bright reflections off the water heat up the atmosphere even here in the shadows of the lunch pavilion. We place our order with the staff and await our meal to be given. What could be possible in this region of grace to receive even more from your plethora of Peace and Joy? I am quiet. This is a blessing beyond measure, this Kamalaya, sanctuary of rest and relaxation where people from all over the world congregate to restore and replenish. I am an observer of this paradise, this moment set in time and place to bring Heaven close to Earth. Today the waves break far from the gentle shore as the heat hangs in the atmosphere over the bay. A blue-gray boulder of granite sits just into the water a few yards creating a sense of safety for the bathers. A man above the dining area plays on a reed flute heavenly tunes that waft through the humid air and bring lightness to our hearts. This is a day that the Lord has made. I will rejoice and be glad in it. All the elements converge to create a perfect tranquility in this compassionate corner of the cosmos. I immerse myself in this inner Joy. I appreciate my destiny which has placed me here. I praise the Divine Mother for Her beauty and grace everywhere amidst this example of Boundless Mercy.

174

The Purpose of This Day

What is the purpose of this day You give? Just as many other days that came before and will come hence, this cycle of light spreads over the Earth as I am awakened. On this sloping forest up from the sea I observe life burgeoning forth in the gentle warmth of the morning sun. A dense blanket of green covers the land, hiding the bungalows in the silence of a concealed order of things. What is this order of the day for me? What foliage spread across my main mountainside would keep the buildings of my Love hidden away in pockets of mystery? These careful constructs of my long-attending craft would best be known—revealed in the true light of their highest function. What purpose did all my former attentions serve? What shelter now to house the people, even myself, and protect them from the stormy weather of strife would emerge as inspiration's home, to be a haven for heavenly states? The purpose of my day is to bring forward that which I have held hidden in the forest of remote expressions, and allow the architecture of my soul's desire to be revealed in its particular structure. Perfectly placed in Your nature, these places that laid hidden in the foliage of earth's nurturing cover now come forth into full function. I walk over the wooden bridge to the entrance of my spacious hall into a cool cover of elegant space. Art and beauty abound in this convergence of Kamalaya— nature enters the heart of my house built for Your Boundless Mercy.

175

A Void That Contains Everything

Evening has come and the dining hour is upon us. The pavilion at Kamalaya is spacious and open, well attended by staff, all gentle in their countenance. The sky is pitch black now as the well-lit space has an aura of bright illumination against a backdrop of a velvety coal horizon. We have placed our order and now relax in this atmosphere of nocturnal aliveness. Our glasses are filled to the brim and remain so. Guests begin to pour in for their night meal. A couple in their 30s sit on the outer edge overlooking the murky black. Dressed in casual clothes, tee shirts and such, they eat their food without much talk. A more elegantly dressed couple at the corner table murmur low sounds and enjoy each other's company. The food seems secondary to their intimate conversation. The long table is filled with middle-aged ladies who congregate in an international sisterhood. Our food arrives one course at a time; the asparagus soup is delicious, just the right starter. My wife eats only half her portion. I finish both dishes. Soon the main dishes are delivered. We switch them around to our original order. Appreciation surrounds us everywhere and is focused now on this meal so well prepared. As we finish, there is no rush to exit. I look again at the velvety black night and apprehend its emptiness—one filled with unseen things. A void that contains everything extends beyond this place of well-appointed comfort. It holds everything in its care, even me, who looks into the blackness of Your Boundless Mercy.

176

Infinity Within Every Instant

Each moment envelops all time and space. There is infinity within every instant. How much greater could my awareness be in this one second? Even the endless elements which compose this scene before me can hardly be noted they are so varied and numerous. Yet in the simplicity of one detail is the living reality of all others. The woven grass placemat on the table at Amrita Café has thousands of knots in rows upon rows, making a field of repeated and intertwined order. My gratitude goes into it like a blessing, and its simple presence sings like a symphony of notes in a sonata of staccato refrains. I sip my coffee in the warm morning light, anticipating my day unfolding. The calm sea is shining in the sun, stretching across the bay to the islands of steep hills covered in forest. Fellow guests sit behind me speaking in German in gentle tones. The bright sunlight illuminates the treetops making a blanket of brilliant green that spreads without end into the distance. A speed boat skids across the surface of the cerulean blue waters. A sound of the reed flute comes through the atmosphere. There is a complete experience of this moment filled with the infinity of things. Beyond awareness, this infinity goes forth unfathomable. Just to ponder this vastness is to be for an instant in my greater Self, the One we share, which is ruler of the Universe. I invoke and praise this Self to make true contact with that State of Mind containing everything in Your Boundless Mercy.

177

Let All Things Be as They Are

I let all things be as they are, falling in place exactly in the perfection of this present moment. The table is before me and like a chessboard the items of breakfast are set in certain order. The grass mats and utensils, the napkins and waterglasses filled with crystal clear water, the grass pressed and embossed menu, the tray with salt and pepper containers—all these to receive our plates of food which come to us from the gentle staff. They bring our coffee too, rounding out the full breakfast. I receive mine with frothy milk in a small beaker. We sit and savor the moment with all the leisure around us, bringing us easily into an inner Joy of contentment. The frothy milk is poured into the coffee cup and brown sugar is sprinkled over the foam. I take a few sips then pause. I eat my scrambled eggs then pause. I observe the other diners then pause. The waiting girls come to remove the plates. Now we are free to go into the rest of our day as we arise from the table of this sacred repast. Walking down the hill to our villa along the narrow path we pass the flowing brook and the groups of tropical trees and plants which make Kamalaya a living paradise. How could we express the Heaven of this encounter with beauty all around us? Letting all things be as they are is to allow Life to flow into me in all its resplendent glory. We are blessed in this reception of Your grace. We are attuned to a life of moment-to-moment awareness of Your Boundless Mercy.

178

This Vision of Holiness

My sight goes forth to see a different world—one of gentleness and peace, one of beauty and grace, one of harmony and aliveness. Inside of me is the Source of this peaceful vision and I would connect with it. This I my choice to do today and every day. Then my vision covers the world with blessings beyond the troubles sometimes found in corners of conflict and strife; pockets of anger, blame, and penalty. Instead, I see the innocence within myself and then in all things around me. The material that makes this cosmos has its beauty and unique variety. The chips of marble form the mosaic, the layer of rocks encircles the veranda, the lawn of green grass extends to the gardens, the foliage of the palms is profuse in its burst of presence. These elements are all endless in presenting Your glory. No end in sight to the material that forms the bank of my poetic abundance. A flag in the distance waves in the wind above the gentle waves lapping onto the beach below. A bather steps cautiously into the water and steadies herself as she moves out into the sea beyond the shore. The sun is brightly reflecting off the water and the ripples shine like jewels in a cluster on the incoming waves. Time slows down to a standstill. My sight goes forth to embrace everything—seen and unseen. What could be excluded from this vision of holiness? I could plant myself anywhere on this planet Earth and find the raw materials that compose Your Boundless Mercy.

179

A Day of Special Blessings

It is a day of special blessings. Life is productive in many ways. Our villa here at Kamalaya is spacious and welcoming. All the cool air blends with this atmosphere of total care. We are amidst the tropical forest which seems as much a part of the architecture as the building itself. Our strong internet connection allows our work to progress as we spend our morning catching up with communications around the world. Soon we go to breakfast in the Soma dining room. This is provided as well in our package of care. I have a plate of raw vegetables, some scrambled eggs, and two cups of coffee. Leisure is the order of the day as all comes to us in the spirit of complete relaxation. We observe the other guests who are relaxing as well in the spacious morning breakfast. Soon we get up and walk back down the hill to our villa. The path is steep, so to the side are steps that make the descent more sure-footed with a handrailing to steady our way down. We enter our villa to the blast of cool air that is very pleasing, a contrast to the hot and humid air of Koh Samui. Again, we sit in our large living room on the couch of comfort checking our Macs for any leftover morning business. The blessings flow in common ways. Nothing particularly stands out as special, yet all is so harmonious and alive that one could say everything is a blessing of monumental proportions. I take it all in and extend an air of gratitude for all that is given. The elements composing all the various things seem so pure and simple: wood is wood, stone is stone, cotton cloth spreads itself across Your Boundless Mercy.

180

Without a Care for a Little While

We are in the mid-day here at Kamalaya, sitting in the small gazebo overlooking the sea. The wind is stronger than usual; therefore, the waves washing up to shore are more vigorous as well. We hear them more frequently in their crashing upon the beach. Awaiting our lunch to be served, I observe the small school of dark striped fish in the pool below and a turtle swimming toward the edge of the pond. There is an air of quiet permeating this idyllic scene as we sit in the peaceful surroundings of the Amrita Café. People speak in low tones and murmurs. The staff in Naples yellow uniforms covers all the stations with a deft attentiveness. We are well cared for in this place of relaxation. The food is prepared as an art and all ingredients are fresh and natural. A holiness in the environment is infused into the meal. It nurtures not only the body but the soul as well. Each dish is like a painting of varied color and texture—with a multi-layered taste coming forth as one eats a total culinary delight. We take our time and slowly savor our lunch amidst the strong sea breezes blowing up from the shore. Even the water takes on an added taste of exceptional quality, served in crystal glasses. We come to the end of our small feast and rise to go back to our villa. Climbing up the steps then through the gardens to the narrow road, we climb the hill to our comfortable home. Glad to be back in the air-conditioned villa, we take our rest in the afternoon and appreciate the freedom just to be without a care for a little while. We give our thanks to be here in Your arms of Boundless Mercy.

181

A Love for Existence

In a new environment at our French Bistro café in Ubud, Bali, we go for the food and air conditioning. It is an ambiance of pleasant surroundings amidst the bustle of Hanuman Street. Many Westerners visit Ubud because they know and feel something different in the atmosphere here. There is a spiritual energy which permeates the space even in the onslaught of Western and commercial influence. I could be anywhere in this world yet will always come back to Bali to relax and replenish body and soul. The Divine Mother is a powerful Force on this "island of the Gods." She is in charge of our time here, which is heavenly in every regard. In this space of divine leisure, all is provided as the Goddesses of Good Fortune bless our every direction and moments. A day has passed, and we have moved to the Lotus Café on the main road. In the open air, we have our lunch overlooking the large lotus pond and the temple behind. People ambulate down the central causeway that divides the pond into two separate bodies of water. Both ponds are covered in the green lotus pads with an occasional shoot of brilliant pinkish orange lotus standing straight and sending a burst of brilliant color into the layer of space above the water. Enthralled by the natural beauty, I allow myself to relax and grow into this Balinese bliss. The sight, sounds, and smell surrounding me is a Love for existence. I am an observer of this Heaven on Earth, this outpouring of Your Boundless Mercy.

182

The Bliss of Bali

The bliss of Bali is all around me in the colors, the textures, the plants, and the people. The sound of running water in the fountain below provides the gentle chorus in this song of Balinese delight. An occasional motorbike whizzes by in the background. Zoom-varoom! It is not out of place in this music of daily living. The clinking of the dishes as the attendant serves our breakfast has a happy ring in our anticipation of our morning coffee and fruit. Ketut, our attendant here at the villas, brings our food lovingly and places each cup, each plate, precisely and carefully on the table. We enjoy the slices of mango and pineapple as we sip our dark brew—the coffee here being one of the strongest in the world. More motorbikes whizz by. Some of the staff speak Balinese in the kitchen below. We anticipate a hot day. Already in the late morning we can feel the heat coming on, even in the shade. Soon we descend the long stairwell to our villa for our morning tasks and communications. In the spaciousness of our cool room we can relax and enjoy the beauty all around us— the peaked ceiling composed of long strands of bamboo with a matting of woven grass in between rises to a crest thirty feet above us; the white chiffon canopy covers our king-sized bed and makes all seem very royal in our world; the bright turquoise water ripples in the pool in front of the deep hunter green rows of plants that make up the private gardens in our walled courtyard. All this a demonstration of Your Bali bliss of Boundless Mercy.

183

Christmas Day

This is Christmas Day in the sanctuary of Your Love. Let us remember the real holy nature of Your mission to awaken us to the truth of who we are. I am Your work in progress of awakening to the Christ in me, as You have a plan for my own enlightenment. Let me not delay any longer in dreams of death, disease, or despair. What is of God belongs to everyone, so please hasten this wakeup call in others as well. I will do my part and play out the true reasons for my Life in the divine plan bigger than myself. In this beauty of Your home, built in the glory of Your adoration, I pray that the powers in charge are transfigured in the truth of Your message. Total innocence abounds in Your Heart which beats as well in the hearts of all. Let guilt be banished forever in this blazing light of Your total absolution. You are the master of complete forgiveness which You bestow generously forever to the entire human race. You are absolute Love incarnate who lights the spark of my True Self to shine in Your glory as well. I claim it here on this day of Christmas. I claim my own Being in this birth of the Son of God within me. No more would I forget or deny who I am. I am the Christ You are, and in this absorption into Truth You impart do we join as real and authentic brothers in the holy dance of Life itself. I give You my body to use in Your service. My eyes and ears are Yours. My hands and feet are Yours, and my mouth can speak Your words now coming from the mutual Father and Mother we Love. I am in Your sanctuary in the full awareness I am here through an act of Your Boundless Mercy.

184

Two Zero Two Zero

Before the New Year, a night out on the town brings us to Blues Alley in Georgetown—an old institution well placed in the annals of famous jazz. "It's fun to go out once in a while," says my consort. It is, especially to the haunts of high art tucked away in an invisible alleyway, attracting some of the best musicians in the field of improvisational sounds. The place fills up early so we came at 6 PM for the eight o'clock show and ordered some drinks and food. A couple nights before New Year's, the energy is already building for the 2020 celebration. It is an auspicious year to be coming down the pike, as not since 1919 has the year had a doubt digit repetition. A melodic number: twenty-twenty, a number formed with 0's and 2's. Twenty, twenty. Two, zero, two, zero. Two together, my lover and me, into the open possibilities of the Great Void, the Divine Zero of unlimited potential to receive whatever manifestation we choose. We put in our order for entrees and await the show. The place is packed by now. We are in the front row with little obstruction of view. On our second beverage, the appetizers already gone, we do our literary things because our daily discussions have run their course. It's a time to hear, to learn, and observe. I scribble down a few lines, look around, then scribble a few more strings of words—much in the same way, I suppose, the jazz man puts his bars of music together. We are anticipating an onslaught of sound that will take us to dimensions unheard of before. I am in this gratitude for the riffs of Your Boundless Mercy.

185

Make Me Like the Wind

Fully in this new year now, would I invoke this other newness to come into my days and make each moment different than the last. What routine could last longer than a second in Your wondrous movement of creation in which the elemental dance of Life is ever unfolding into the present? No two moments are the same. No two years are the same in human history. In 2020 there is a cycle complete—101 years since 1919. And before that year, another 101 years since 1818. The repetitions go on. Yet what in me does not repeat in this Life unique? Would my heart beat the same as the minute just before? Would I suddenly forget my speech and talk in tongues of a different era? What meanders take me around to new bends and flows in the stream of my essential actions? I ask You, Divine Mother of Newness Itself, to place me in the forefront of Your outpouring of Beauty. In this second of arrival, keep me moving to the next, and then the next again. Make me like the wind which blows over hill and dale without touching the same location twice. Let me give my blessings upon the cheeks of walkers and talkers and lift the loose leaves on the forest floor to make them fly through the breeze of Nature's beatitude. I am in the moment now of a Joy unsurpassed. I am in the dalliance with matter in Your Boundless Mercy.

186

At Peace with Myself

In the atmosphere of Pure Joy, I relinquish duality. What I observe then is enveloped by the acceptance of Your Love. Not one thing is out of place when this stillness is felt and applied to all things around me. In the waiting room for an appointment, the television is blaring with a talk show. I cannot turn it off. The African American woman is animated, discussing a current epidemic—a virus in from China. People there are in quarantine; here the buzz is caution. Experts say, "Don't worry." The show moved on to discuss mental health, or lack of it. Many on the street are stuck in the confusion of bipolar illness. The host, in a beige skirt and red blouse, showed true care for all her subjects. Then, a break for a commercial. The time goes on by and we move to a different department. The world these days is divided into parts. We are divided into parts, but really a wholeness abounds without this division and fragmentation. A different world emerges. The sights and sounds have their own beauty that infiltrates my perception and removes any judgments that linger around my vision. I am given a great gift of Your method of sight—one of gentleness and peace, one of harmony and aliveness. It does not matter what is before me. I borrow Your eyes and ears which only bless the impressions they are receiving. There is an air of quiet hovering around my encounters with everything. I can be at peace with myself in this movement through a collision of unrelated elements. It is my call to bring order to the appearances of chaos. The harmony of what is present invokes Your Boundless Mercy.

187

A Convergence of Souls

It is night and I await a convergence of souls to come in morning's light—a meeting in which illusions disappear in the great shining of Your Love. Five brothers and sisters come to awaken into the reality of their Holy Self. Let all things be exactly as they are. Let the past be forgotten, or the gems of memory be set in the crown of present glory. We are of royal majesty, so why pretend to be marooned to a lower fate, one of limitation and doubt. Nowhere has God put me in the prison of a self-imposed guilt, bereft of the cosmic innocence I am. So would my friends in holiness rise up into the Self we share. By Your mercy would we let go of our burdens, making the case of our being so light that it may ascend into another realm of delight You grant to us. Let us be clear of what could never be: a separation only imagined in the hell we made up. Place us at nirvana's gate. Give us the push we need to step though this old unwillingness to claim our ascension into heaven. Now are we one with the essence of our Source; now are we joined with the purpose of our life; now are we fully present with no tinge of doubt; now are we in the momentum of our sacred reality that dawns inside our heart's full power. What else is there left to do in this night of anticipation amidst the promise of Your Boundless Mercy?

188

These Times of a Viral Scare

I am at home as most people are in these days of self-quarantine. A global shutdown has occurred. Could it ever be imagined? Something that seems "out of the blue" could be in the natural order of things. Could Mother Earth be telling us to reboot and give up our fearful and frenetic ways? What are these unusual times telling us? What are you doing here? surviving? Why are you in this life? to pay rent? This is a test of faith. The ways of before are no longer pertinent to the present. The purpose of life is no less important than before—and perhaps more urgently these times demand we know that real purpose full on. To remember God in actuality is my function here through forgiveness that is total. God is the only goal I have today. Let me remember that my goal is God. What greater need than this confronts my days? There is an attention I give to things. In this one great need would I turn my attentions to the Divine in me. God is the strength in which I trust, so let me be in touch with that real Power that flows through me. There is no Source but this, and nothing lives in this world without the spark of God's Love giving it Being. I have time to make this connection that does not require time. There is a lot of space to feel the Love of God within me now. What would God have me do? Say what and to whom? Go where but here? I am alert to a new, all-pervasiveness. You surround me with Your Love. Allow me to receive it in full awareness. In these times of a viral scare, let Your Truth fill me with Boundless Mercy.

189

In This Great Sequester

"This is the day the Lord has made. We will rejoice and be glad in it. Make a joyful noise unto the Lord." I sing the praises of the Divine Father, Mother, and Child in these times of the Great Sequester. I look out my windows to a forgiven world and see the beauty of all the common things, quiet and still, that form my neighborhood of orderly buildings and streets. Only a few vehicles come down the road. I hear the swoosh of the heat coming out of the ducts high above. I appreciate the lofty ceiling in our apartment many feet higher than the usual height. We are blessed by this spaciousness of our holy home You provide for us. It is filled with reminders of Your Love. We have an altar in every room, a vortex of Your Divine Energy filling our space with the blessings of Your Eternal Care for us. We have a large kitchen table with an oak top on which I do my work. I can be in the flow of listening and responding to Your call to action of various tasks of my morning. I am in the Love You are, and my Identity is shared in abundance through my day in the communications You prompt me to make. In this Great Sequester, all is well in my world. I am Self-reliant, receiving the inspirations You intend for me. I am cleansed of my fear and doubt as I move forward into the new. I am blessed in the present with infinite possibilities. I cannot forget Your Presence that surrounds me with Your certain care of Boundless Mercy.

190

The Right Approach

We went for a walk, the first in three weeks for me. The cool atmosphere merited a jacket. I wore my orange ski, zipper in the front, the one I bought in Colorado. It was a brisk walk, wind blowing in sharp gusts down toward the baseball stadium along the river boardwalk. I was wearing my black ostrich cowboy boots, so the heels made their staccato taps on the boards. A few dog walkers were out. Some had masks and some did not. I wore one for the first time, with an American flag pattern. The thing made my glasses steam up. I got used to it, though I would have felt just as safe without it. Sometimes conforming and going along with what others feel is safer is the right approach. Why add more pushback to a situation already wrought with fear and distrust? That would not be wise. So, I wore my mask with an element of glee, all the time appreciating the new spring growth that abounds all around us now. The seasons turn and churn just as they always have; not one casualty of the COVID-19 has affected Your Love. Not one has died without that vibration in their makeup already. There are no victims here. What can be attracted will be attracted by those with a lower vibration that matches the place of least resistance. People who wish to die will do so for various reasons. Perhaps John Prine was simply "ready to go," and so he did via the COVID-19. I am in my day now, awaiting our call with Brazil in an hour or so. What will we say? There is a music playing over the air waves of Your Boundless Mercy.

191

In the Ocean of Devotion

"What could there be in me that needs forgiveness when Yours is perfect? The sleep of forgetfulness is only my unwillingness to remember Your forgiveness and Your Love." (ACIM) The cleansing of my mind is my responsibility in the ocean of devotion to Life's Love. God is Life and Life is Love, therefore, God is Love. A pure appreciation for Life is to Love, and therefore to be connected in our Source to God. People have lost faith because they have lost the ability to appreciate. In the Great Sequester we are given the opportunity to "do less" and appreciate more. The only thing we need to correct in ourselves is this tendency to forget our eternal gratitude. It is not hard to appreciate life. What is "hard" is to not appreciate the things that allow us to be here. I love the air, the water, the heat of the sun, the body of my muse, the soft and supple places that grip me in a loving embrace of eternal and holy care. My needs are met by these Divine Forces which create universes. Why would I be any less than a sun which shines its light for billions of years? Divine Mother of all things, I am the Son You Love. Let me not give back anything less to You than a Cosmos of compassion. You awaken me to my Holy Self that I may enliven it with Action. I show up in my movements of adoration of all that is given in infinite abundance. The way is clear, and the path is easy to accept Your Love. This morning is full of new food for my soul in this spirit pantry of Your Boundless Mercy.

192

The Peace of God

It is mid-morning here in Washington. I have checked my emails to find nothing cataclysmic. Nothing too inspiring either. Now I am wondering what to do. The sound of the refrigerator motor goes on in the background. My wife is at her desk in the second bedroom, transfixed at her Mac writing with recently gained intensity a new book: *The Supermarket for a Meaningful Life*. A few cars and trucks rumble down the street. The atmosphere is bright but not totally clear as the sky is a shade of silvery whitish gray with just the slightest tinge of powder blue. I count my blessings. The large oak-topped table holds all my office things in this spacious great room. It is my command central. I try to keep it neat, but sometimes it stacks up into a semblance of mild chaos. I trust all things will line up okay. In this Great Sequester I have the space to see things differently. Sometimes a tinge of fear crosses my mind: What am I to do? What am I to say and to whom? The actions that I take are totally up to me. I can make another video. What will I say and why? Better to be silent now and let the Peace of God take over. The river does not wonder where it is going. The bird does not look at a map. The Earth revolves for eons without concern. Why should I give pause to notice anything except Your eternal care for me? I sit down to write this ode in the space of the ever-present Now. Let each instant suffice that I may observe Your glory and place my trust in receiving Your Boundless Mercy.

193

This Sunday of Natural Peace

Sunday has its natural peace. We are absorbed in the quiet I so much adore. The silence of the sound of God includes all noises and rustles that compose the sonata of daily life. I can hear the scratching of this pen across the paper page in my odes to Boundless Mercy. I can sense the dim ticking of the large clock that leans against the backsplash of tiles behind the stove. I hear the motor of the refrigerator humming in the background. The tablescape holds the dear things that inhabit my common world. I am not concerned with chaos, nor with an order I construct from pieces of this or that. There is a universal order that has nothing to do with my attempts to harmonize the things around me. What I see and hear and touch are small players in the Cosmic play of galaxies hurling through space at the speed of light. I am a small unit in the grand design of things, attempting not to harm all that bumps up against me. Let me be unaffected by any thoughts that hurt. We walk a line in regions we cannot comprehend, yet would all the things along the way reveal Your very nature to us and make us ever grateful to be opening our eyes to a different reality—one of beauty and grace of all You have given. On this Sunday of natural peace, there is an appreciation for domestic blessings of Your Boundless Mercy.

194

The Place Where We Join

We are in the swing of our work, adapting it to the Great Sequester. Today we spoke to people in Denmark and offered them a breathe. This connection over the ethers is a new realm of freedom. The mind is the place where we join, and in this realization of oneness space and time are rendered less a block of limitation than dimensions of real unity. A gladness sweeps over me in the company of people with whom we come together in this wholeness. They look at their computer screens and we look back at them. The little thumbnail pics of them, all in neatly placed rows, give us a sense of the presence in this time we share together. Praise God for creating Zoom through the mind of some tech genius. We can reach people all around the globe and give them our words of comfort, our gift of Liberation Breathing, our hearts of pure Joy. You make the air waves clear for our signal to go out to the universe without impediments. You bring the people we are meant to reach in this heart connection. Help me to speak and show only Your truth. Let me be in the Joy of receiving and giving. Keep all untruths away from my mind, knowing You are the Truth that burns away the remains of my ego that does not serve Your Will for my total liberation. Let my mind move in the direction of Your Love in this Great Sequester. Let all corrections be made in the order of Your Boundless Mercy.

195

Om Namah Shivay

It is another Sunday morning, and we are up before sunrise. After the morning shower and dressing, I sit at the kitchen table to have my Italian brew. The coffee is warm and comforting. My wife is saying her Om Namah Shivays on the living room couch. I ponder and bless communications from the day before. Some of them required my correction. Attention to the details of a past I had made revealed an untruth. I was embarrassed for having put it out. Correction must be a love within to keep all untruths away from my thought. Picking up the pieces of my hurt ego, I fixed what I could to move on. Now I am in the aftermath of the sting. The small untruths are just as off as the large ones—a lesson in discrimination was flunked so now would I revisit my own ignorance of insensitivity. The snake around the neck of Shiva is a serious thing, but only after the truth of his immunity to the poison. He transcends his ego to rise above the dramas of thought, of fear of death, of conflict between factions, of good or evil in the scheme of human existence. He sits on Kailash to be free of all suffering. The snakes come to him for warmth, which he gives. Om Namah Shivay is the honoring of His name. To speak it is to be in his vibration of destruction, to be cleansed of all untruths of word or deed. Om Namah Shivay is putting one's Self in the crucible of cleansing, in the smelter of an inferno which burns away all inappropriate gestures in the care of Boundless Mercy.

196

Engineered Over Time

The middle of the week stirs with activity on the street. The construction company has begun their maneuvers in the next block on the new apartment building started last year. Machinery is banging and clanging in the noise of big movements. We are still in this Great Sequester, observing the general life of our neighborhood gradually returning. Slowly coming back into focus, moving in the direction of a teeming activity of joy. I am here at the kitchen table scribing this ode, listening to the sound of the refrigerator motor in the white noise of its hum. The day is before me in its splendor of unlimited possibilities. Some meetings are planned for which we are glad. The internet platforms let us see people in Denmark and Holland. What praises could I sing to You, Divine Mother of the ethers Who makes this communication possible? Engineered over time You bring the know how into the minds of humanity to end this separation that was going on for eons. We are One, and You are now awakening us to that fact. Zoom at the speed of light Your words of encouragement to Your children who are finally listening for Your Love. We have taken pause from the incessant distractions that kept our awareness separated from Your Eternal Love. Now it is blazing in all things, and we see You in the sights and sounds of nature, in the objects of crystal-clear beauty that inhabit our earthly kingdom of right here and now. In this middle of the week I am elated to be in the sight of Your Boundless Mercy.

197

The Divine Mother's Angels

I started a fast today. The times are right for a raise in vibration. I am requesting to receive a certainty of purpose to know the truth.: I am sustained by the love of God. The body has enough stored fat to last me a long time, so putting more substance in my body right now is not so necessary. And to turn back the aging process takes a commitment to a more actual Divine Connection. So much of the time our belief takes us over, and what is actual is a resignation to the status quo that falls short of our total liberation from death. The mere idea of immortality does not mean we will realize it in this lifetime. It is said, "Only the Divine Mother grants the boon of Physical Immortality." I accept the truth of this statement. So, what is my right relationship with the Divine Mother? Jesus in his Essene Gospel of Peace refers to the Divine Mother's angels: fire (light), air, water, earth, space (ether). I start with direct relationship with these. Light, air, and then water are the most essential in the fast. One cannot live in the dark without light, air, or water. Five minutes without air, one would be dead. A few days without water, one would begin to physically decline. These are the angels sent by the Divine Mother to cleanse us, to save us, to liberate us from death. Will we take advantage of this ancient wisdom or just sluff it off as more myth? This is my test right now. I am using myself as an experiment in truth. Now I rely solely on Your Boundless Mercy.

198

Joy is Always Present

The present is always full of Joy, the promise of perpetual Life, the blessings of our Creator bestowed upon us. Are we absent in our unawareness of the present? One breath is enough to be grateful for because Life itself is a great gift. The breath connects us to this present. The work of this day is to bring myself closer to this state of total appreciation and gratitude for this Life I have. In the Great Sequester I have more space just to be still in a state of peace. The divine providence that is always around is no different now than it is anytime. My Life on Earth is a continuum of other lives on Earth long past and yet to come. Yet it is always my Life right now in which I must find my joy. It is always present, yet sometimes I am absent when my attention is directed wrongly away from Pure Joy. Why would I allow my mind to wander off in feelings of a dissatisfied despair? All cause for gratitude emerges here in this holy moment. It contains universes of reasons to be happy. Let me embrace these reasons and feel the Love of God within me now. I am given everything to bring Joy. The vibration of our living space is elevated so there is no cause for doubt or fear. I can choose peace instead of the doldrums of despair that are mere indulgences of unwillingness to accept myself as God created me to be. Let me awaken from this sleep of unwillingness and be in the creative flow of my real destiny now. All is well in my world even in this unusual time at home. An opportunity for ascension is present. I am stepping into higher levels of Boundless Mercy.

199

The Mantra of You

I am saying the mantra of You, Divine Mother of the Universe. The vibration of rejoicing comes into me and I feel the Love of God surrounding my space. You give me countless reasons to be engulfed with gratitude. So why are there times in which the blues get the better of me? Let me stay out front of my Joy. Let me take these things in stride amongst the infinite details of the day and acknowledge the greater parts of myself that feel Your love and care. Help me to desist from mental grumbling in which I am going a different direction from Your Will for me. I observe the beauty very easily all around me. The oak wood on this tabletop has a grain that is pleasing to my eyes. Other things as well attract my grateful gaze. The blue glass water bottles have a stalwart presence as they hold our drinking water in a special place of purification. My Mac is a beautiful thing as well. It connects me to the world and, broader still, to the universe. Divine Love and wisdom are all around me, so why not tap into them moment to moment in my dance of daily existence? Why would I maintain even the slightest gap between me and Pure Joy? There is none in reality. So, as I pay homage to You, Divine Mother of my greatest Joy, help me to be only as You created me. Allow my Life to flow and receive in the directions You appointed for me in the beginning of time. I am the vessel of Your Love on this new earth of Boundless Mercy.

200

The Work of the Day

This day of computing is all but done. Why are we so tied to our electronic devices in this age? Much time we are tied to them it seems. Communication channels are increased, yet to what ends? What is the message? No longer does the medium suffice. I dig deeply into myself for something meaningful to say. There is a peace and joy that is determined to stay focused on higher matters. The work of the day to contact these feelings of happiness is the most important endeavor in my life. The external conditions are not the determiners of how I feel, but rather how I feel attracts the external conditions I wish to see. In an ocean of Joy, how is it that I can feel deprived or ever down? The work of the day has its actions. Are they taken from a place of infinite love and gratitude? My needs are totally met in this moment. Our life is productive in our relationships around the world. Our living space is beautiful and satisfying. There is adequate supply. We have something to give. All the external elements are well situated, yet am I feeling as high as I should in this intention to fully awaken? Salvation is my only function in this world of separation from the Absolute. Always present, the Peace of God surrounds me fully without end. There is no time or space in which it is absent. Am I absent from it? This is my job and work of the day: to use my time on my computer to awaken fully to Joy in this ocean of Your Boundless Mercy.

201

In the Environment of Joy

This is the day that the Lord has made. I will rejoice and be glad in it. There are joyful noises all around me and I am engulfed in them. There are magnificent sites that inspire my blessings. My needs are more than met in this universe that has no lack. What cares could I have in this life of Divine Providence? The work of the day is to appreciate my good fortune. The gratitude for all that exists shows up in my particulars. Spaciousness abounds in our gracious apartment with high ceilings. The art objects we own are eclectic in the energy they transmit. The down-pillowed couch is inviting comfort into our home. Our entryway is flanked by sculptures and paintings of the Divine Mother which raise the vibration of all who enter. We have an altar in every room, so the frequency of holiness is certain in our sacred space. We work on our Macs which connect us to the world. Our shelves are well stocked, and our refrigerator is full. The view from our windows is spectacular, so we are in the environment of JOY. This is a special day of peace. I am without concerns for the future because I place it in Your Hands. I hear the construction sounds outside that fill the atmosphere with noise, and the loud trucks that bring their materials to the site. This does not disturb the Peace that emanates forth from Your Love which is in every molecule of my own amazement. This noise is joyfully in Your Boundless Mercy.

202

The Epitome of Creation

We are coming to the end of the Great Sequester, so the forays into the outside world are more frequent. Today I mailed a painting to foreign lands in hopeful expectation it will arrive safely. The painting was new, hardly birthed into being, and different from any done before. Would this not be the epitome of creation? From unknown forces comes something not yet named or quite understood, yet there it is in the fullness of its being, staring me in the face. I look back in wonder; where is it from? where is it going? what meaning does it have for me and those who take pause to look at it? It is out in the world now. How could this be when months before it did not even exist? I surrender to a creative Power beyond myself, yet fully grounded within my Self. I follow its promptings onward. Where but into this fertile future could I throw my attentions, into this fervent longing to reveal something never before revealed? I proceed in the increments of one gesture at a time, one color considered, one layer upon layer that often ends in the obliteration of much that came before. I follow the creative trail without looking back at an apparent loss. Loss is not loss when properly perceived. I sent a painting out today to Latvia, there on the Baltic Sea, to a Viking lady of stature, one of apparent nobility of Spirit who understands these things. "Orchid, Butterfly, Purple Heart, Mountain and Water" compose Your Boundless Mercy.

203

The Real Pulse of Creation

Within these few rooms for months, I begin to see a universe in the Great Sequester inside myself. What could that be like when my body in the world is no longer needed, yet that part of me that ever continues is still intact? It extends even farther beyond this small Earth and enters galaxies of stars beyond the mere reach of human effort. In these times at home would my Being come into its own with no real comparison to what it should do, or could do, or would in the end do. No "doing" was necessary. But neither would slovenly idleness be the order of the day; always something of an inspiration to extend, a beauty to notice, a communication to be made. These actions come naturally to any person alive, more so when the superfluous movements cease and only the real work of the day brings Love ever closer to my full awareness. It would take this long respite from activity to find the real pulse of creation. This beating of the heart of Life itself is always throbbing in the bosom of my Divine person, yet too busy to notice and feel the graciousness of a daily blessing, my preoccupations kept me ever absent from receiving it. No more would this be the case. Adequately slowed down to be in the Home of Your Love, I discover it is my own. I give myself this space beyond the stars and feel the expansion of my soul amidst Your Boundless Mercy.

204

Deeper Than A Virus

A backlash of COVID-19 sweeps across our nation as perhaps we took confidence for granted and threw caution to the wind. Yet a disease is deeper than a virus that infects the human race. Some places like Japan and New Zealand have hardly any cases, keeping their thoughts and their people clear of conflict, fear, and confusion. And we, in the battle-ridden zones of the American media, cannot seem to rise above the turmoil—inner and outer— polarized to no ends in the incessant clamor of clashing views. We call ourselves "democratic," yet this seems to manifest as freedom to scratch and squabble to the top of the heap—the platform with most reach to the rabble rousing of a noisy world. But the microcosm aligns with the macrocosm at hand. A virus in the social order of things comes from the deeper virus in our souls, then that manifests as a bug. Bugs are everywhere. God bless them. Say another Om Namah Shivay and put the lid on the trash can. Throw out the bath water of conflict and doubt but keep the baby of our truly cleansed innocence. We are still here at home and we can be in the momentum of Grace beyond our understanding. Why engage in the system that has yet to sort itself out? We can do what we choose in the flux of God's will. Why worry or plan to go hither and tither in the Great Sequester which is apparently not yet complete? We make a joyful noise in Boundless Mercy.

205

On This Plateau of Plenty

I am at the table of Your Love that has a multi-function. In the center of our home, it is a place where all are fed. Mostly, it is where I am fed. I write my odes here, I paint the small watercolors of brilliant colors here, I sit to eat my breakfast here, I work on my Mac and send all the communications that happen in my day. On this plateau of plenty, I experience the cornucopia of Your care and receive Your certain gifts that fill my life with the elements that sustain me. In this Great Sequester I spend my days at this table of Your Love and notice what comes and goes. We have clients over Zoom, and I set up the ring light, so our faces are well lit. Our computers are plugged in and function at their optimum. The mail from our box sits on the corner of the table awaiting opening. A book I ordered on Amazon is still unopened, yet to be read. The small recorder we use to capture our talks awaits the next lecture. My Apple earphones are gathered in a twisted entanglement of wires. The empty coffee cup sits on the coaster with cookie crumbs scattered around it from my morning crumpet. I am in the momentum of appreciation for even these crumbs of compassion which cross into my tablescape of poetic scrutiny. I look and then touch these tidbits forming a scene on this plateau of the oaken boards which hold Your Boundless Mercy.

206

The Unfolding of our Days

We are outside at a local restaurant having a celebration of sorts, just to be out and about in this Great Sequester. The July summer day is warm but not too warm, and a slight breeze moves the air as we sit at this table by the boardwalk. The waiter wears a mask, and we do as well until our beverages arrive to our delight. The normal functions of life are no longer taken for granted. Just this simple act is a special joy in the unfolding of our days. I have a Bavarian dark beer, rich in flavor, smooth and well-crafted from a brewery that started in 1878. I take my time sipping in the deliciousness of this moment. What time can go by that universal forces do not notice? There is no crisis that the Cosmos recognizes as real. Just a virus in the scheme of things. Souls come and go, in and out of bodies for many other reasons as well—a natural occurrence in the dance of Life. I choose to stay manifested. Let not my subconscious mind conjure an affiliation with this COVD-19. Let not disease or death take my attentions in the momentum of fear that sweeps the news. I am the sovereign of my destiny in this time of trials. I cannot be subject to a will not my own, therefore a victim of circumstances beyond my control I am not. Let me stay in the momentum of Pure Joy. I ask God, my Creator, to free me from the bondage of subconscious thought and memories that replay as problems. I ask for the Heaven state now, in this real world of Your Boundless Mercy.

207

The Sky Will Not Fall

I arise to another day. The actions are very similar to every day: say my prayer; make the bed; read my Ode to You, Divine Mother of the Universe; check my text messages; grab my cup of coffee; shave and shower; put on my clothes spread across the bed the night before by my lover; put on my watch and "Om Namah Shivay" bracelets; stick my Little Hanuman in my pocket, and away I go. What next? I usually do not have an agenda, and I am guided. Today I am writing first in the book of Your Boundless Mercy and pondering the meaning of Your presence in my life. What is this mercy that transcends all lower orders of care? The elements are provided. I need not worry that I will run out of air. The water has always been in abundance. Not one day of my life has the sun ceased to shine. And on those rainy days of doldrums would I remain certain of Your light behind my clouds and the hope of a bright day would always return to me. I have never missed a meal unless I chose to skip it. My bills have always been paid, so why should I worry and fret that the "sky may fall"? It will not. It cannot, even amid apparent turmoil. The only upheavals are inside of me. Fear is not justified, yet do I still indulge in concern for the future when the present is all just fine. Dear Cosmic Mother of all time and space, still my mind and bring peace to my soul. You are the Great Care that never ceases to tend to Your endless creation with Boundless Mercy.

208

Beside the River's Edge

In the late July atmosphere beside the river's edge, we take our leisure. Day after day spent inside gives me an impetus to bust out of these four walls of confinement into the outer space at large. We sit at a small round table with our beverages poured into glasses we brought along with us. It is a kind of mini picnic of sorts. The chirping sparrows hop about in search of crumbs. Passersby are wearing their masks as we enjoy sitting, relaxing, observing, and writing in our journals of supreme gratitude. I am drinking a Belgian ale from the Abbey of Leffe, founded in the year 1240. That is 780 years of continuous ale production coming across the great water to this place in Washington in the year of our Lord, 2020. I am glad to have this time of outdoor respite. What plagues swept over the Old World are now in this new form of COVID-19 disrupting these modern times of the internet age. I check Facebook on my iPhone. This is the way it is in this virtual world. I notice the new arches forming the bridge constructed downstream are coming more into shape. A beautiful structure of three double sets of arches crosses the Anacostia River in our town. They go from Washington to Arlington and make the transition smooth and beautiful. I observe in this last day of July 2020 with my Belgian ale, a beauty of the Divine unsurpassed. What but this "plague" of the modern pandemic could instigate a Great Sequester in which these beautiful scenes of observation are made known in this ocean of local Boundless Mercy.

209

Down to Rise Up

Take me to the river, down again by the tranquil flow of Your liquid Love of natural beauty. The tables and chairs are set for our enjoyment. We are in the shade of the nearby mountain ash tree across from the docks that hold slick boats and modest yachts. The breeze creates a pleasant atmosphere on this early August day. The air is clean, and people are sauntering up and down the boardwalk. A couple with an infant stroller embraces their baby and has a picnic on the grass. Reggae music is playing in the background from one of the outdoor restaurants in the neighborhood. The late afternoon light begins to cast long shadows and the shade of the tree is extended even farther across the park lawn. A group of young girls talk together at the table next to us. Very animated, they are happy in their cool summer attire—shorts and tank tops—scantily dressed for the heat. Their conversation is dynamic. "Oh, hell no, they know better!" I hear one exclaim with gestures that make her point known. All is building the community of folks around us who make up this point pleasant of our urban setting. We are blessed by the beauty of your Love, by the flow of the wide river, by the green of the long grass lawn, by the caress of Your gentle breezes, by the ripples of moving water on the surface of aqua expanse, by the conversations of people having fun in their human element. We come down here to the river, down to rise up in Your Boundless Mercy.

210

A Joy Just to Be

We are outside in the free atmosphere of reason. Nature has an order that cannot contradict the Divine reality of Joy, and in this consistent beauty is there a logic of Love that prevails in every situation. We sit at our small table by the marina. A river view graces us with visions of tranquility. The boats, large and small, are docked in their berths awaiting their next voyage. A small craft darts upstream in the distance. The drone of the city makes its hum of deep urban sound in the background, most likely the muffled roar of the interstate that cuts through southern D.C. Voices of the bicyclers call from down below on the boardwalk. "What is it?" I hear, as I sip my Belgian beer. A loud crash is heard from the construction site behind us—metal dumpsters are being off-loaded. The three-part bridge is going up nicely downstream, each complete row with its double arch. A family rests at another table wearing their masks, having a lively conversation about something. It is a joy just to be. In the leisure of the day we can disengage from computers and mobile devices long enough to appreciate a few breaths of fresh air. I am as God created me, along with the trees, the river, the man-made architecture of the Divine Mother's materials. I write down what I see and hear, but in no way is this all there is. Your infinite universe converges in the point where I am, and blessings flow to me regardless of particular elements of Your Boundless Mercy.

211

Nothing is Less and Nothing is More

We are in the Joy of our day. There is a peace that envelopes us in this space around this perch over the river. The sleek boats rest in their slips and anticipate their course across the water. I am in awe of the beauty of the natural elements of land, water, spacious atmosphere, and architectural elements well designed. We are on a plateau of granite pavers above the boardwalk below. On this table we write our words of natural adorations. Nothing is less and nothing is more in the perfection of this moment. There is a space of receptivity that does not project, does not preconceive a trajectory of telling phrases. What is present comes to me without effort or plan. The parents of a restaurant owner sit at the table next to us. We greet them in a gentle fashion as we spread out our tablecloth over the adjacent grouping of table with chairs. None of the time we spend out and about is confined to an agenda. We are free to relax and observe and allow Your day to unfold and be as it is. The warmth of this August day envelops us as the breeze coming off the water keeps the heat in moderation. We are enjoying this caring from Your elements. What would lend more perfection to this scene that You have not already provided? I receive this blessing of our neighborhood— our Navy Yard—in which the river is a prominent player in the local dynamic of a wonderful Life immersed in Your Boundless Mercy.

212

The Night Lingers On

At home in the night. Again, I am here with myself in this moment of observation in the presence of Your all-pervasive quiet. The sound I have heard a thousand times before—the drone of the refrigerator—is ever in the background. The AC unit pushes the cool air through the ductwork above. I am well-lit on the couch, looking to the right at the Divine Mother altar and Her representative objects. What could be Your will for me in this suspension of all doing? Language falls short in these descriptions of where I am. There is a great presence of things all around, most humble in their silence, never pushing themselves forward to be noticed. Yet I notice them. They are the common things around our house. A wooden trunk with the carved immortalists is in front of me. A few things rest on its top: a coaster, a couple books, the recorder, and a glasses case. Farther off is the kitchen table with all the chairs around it and things on it and things under it. We have a high ceiling of concrete above us, with pipes, ducts, and wire conduits exposed in the style of loft architecture we love. I have a computer plugged in nearby. So glad to be handwriting in this book; could it even take place this day and age? Are children even taught to write out their words, or is the keyboard the only thing they know in this digital age? I could be resting now in a different space of truth. I see what I see and hear what I hear. The night lingers on and my eyes get heavy toward a sleep of Your Boundless Mercy.

213

In the Flow

On a Friday night, the work of the week comes to a close. It is time to relax and appreciate the Divine leisure bestowed on us. We go outside and walk down to the marina overlook. Our table is there, and we set up shop for a beverage and time to read and write. The August sun is going down in the western sky as the gentle breeze brushes over our cheeks and our hair is gently blown toward the coolness of a late summer day. We are blessed in this time of the Great Sequester to be in the flow of Your Service. We have a mission which is naturally unfolding in its own way, and we are immensely gratefully for the Divine Providence which meets all our needs. There is no dearth of opportunity into which we move and work in a new way. We flow into the unspoken realms of grace, into a Love beyond reason, into the care which meets our needs before we even know we have them. I observe the happenings of this world in a different light. Everything is a wonder, all happenings a miracle, each encounter a holy blessing. What could there be in me that needs forgiveness, when Yours is perfect. We sit at our table and enjoy this creative atmosphere of Pure Joy, of unlimited possibilities for a holy future. We are certain of Your Love, which is also our own. The boats in their slips sit silently in the Presence of the own beauty. The boardwalk receives the happiness of passersby. I am in the momentum of Life unending from the glory of Your Boundless Mercy.

214

A Magnet for More

The late afternoon sun begins to descend in the western sky as we sit at our table by the marina. The restaurants are open now—at least outside—and the music blasts over the loud speakers. We started bringing a red checkered tablecloth to spruce up our round top and feel the true elegance of the situation. We are blessed in the abundance of this moment outside of time. Two boats slowly putter upstream then one of them stops and turns completely around, headed in the opposite direction. The second boat eventually turns around as well. A square houseboat comes along slowly and disappears in the distance. Other neighbors have their take-out at the tables around us. The relaxed atmosphere contributes to our inner Joy. There is no end to it. We are here in this time and space zone to be happy; all else is meaningless futility. The cause for Joy is so close—closer than our own breath. When this contact is made, all the pleasant visions of Love race to be in the center of this wondrous whirl of attraction. All the items in our spiritual pantry of Divine Providence line up for our well-being. This gratitude for good feelings is a magnet for more positive aspects of our lives. The scenes of our cool neighborhood increase. One thing after another that makes us feel Joy lines up in anticipation of our acceptance. We allow the good things to flow to us. The long shadows of the late Washington day extend their grace into the marina of Your Boundless Mercy.

215

In the Grace of Late Summer

Sunday afternoons are the epitome of Divine leisure. We have the space to relax and be in the grace of late summer. The weather is cooling down and the cicadas are making their shrill buzzing sounds in the trees. We go to our spot in the shade overlooking the marina and boardwalk and spread our checkered tablecloth over the small round top. Others are happy in the gentle breeze to be out and about on this clear and cloudless day. We sit and have a beverage, another mini picnic of sorts, in this relaxed atmosphere of early September. I can appreciate our neighborhood for having such a beautiful environment for people to enjoy. We count our great blessings to be placed in this holy zone of wellbeing, in the capital of our nation. In this Great Sequester, the environment of beauty is very important as it engulfs all the elements in its confluence of creation: the mountain ash trees sway gently in the swirl of a breeze; the people gather in isolated groups on the grassy lawn that spreads one hundred yards to the east; the medium-sized yachts are docked at their slips on the water's edge; the new bridge downstream is coming together with its triple arches. It is time to be glad for all that is given in this day of sacred and silent rejoicing. I make a joyful noise without sound inside my heart to the God who keeps all things great and wonderful. You spread Your infinite elements before me in the sensual feast of scenes which compose Your Boundless Mercy.

216

One Life Abounds

In the middle of this week I am immersed in a new pondering. The Great Sequester goes on, but people are out and about with and without masks. It is as if we are totally fed up with this viral threat, even if it remains to hold some sway over our fears. We are close to saying "go to hell" to the whole matter and take our chances with fate as we throw ourselves into the ocean of Joy all around us. Could happiness be the best immunity? What would pure joy do for the physics of my body? I give attention to this moment of beauty, which is here now, and allow its elemental part to take over my whole. One Life abounds forever in all directions emanating outward from my center of awareness. I find myself writing these words in an Italian journal with a mechanical pencil, listening to the sounds of my thoughts, hearing the subtle scratching noise that comes from the flow of graphite over the paper surface of the page. The clock on the stove ticks on. I notice it is almost midnight. It is quiet on the street, and in our apartment even more so. An occasional car goes down the road. I use the eraser on the end of the pencil to erase a misspelled word. Fortunately, not many changes are needed in these outbursts of scribbling. What I would like to say is that which one says when he does not know what to say. There is no shortage of words when silence is present in my heart. Nothing is ignoble—not one thought is superfluous when attention is paid to the all-pervasive sacredness of this moment. Words come alive in Your Boundless Mercy.

217

The Conglomerate of Conditions

I am attentive to the heaven that is right now. Beauty is infused into all the small details of my work. The threads of the black and red tablecloth are woven together in a bold checkered plaid. The evening light casts its long shadows across the boardwalk below. The small yellow leaves collect on the steps in a long formation, shapeshifting in the gentle breeze. The golden leather bag sits on the empty chair. Two young men converse with lively gestures twenty feet away. The restaurant is busy with outdoor guests who sit amidst the beat of the bass drum playing loudly over the speakers. The fall atmosphere is upon us, sending a cold chill across the back of my neck. It is jacket weather now, even on this day of Indian summer. The large boats in the marina line up in rows from the dock, catching the early evening light, shining a brilliance not seen on any other object in this scene. A man wearing headphones does his yoga on the grass lawn below. Here I am still writing, looking, feeling, and noticing the next thing to describe in this ode. What composes heaven but the common things of our day? The conglomerate of conditions and things are ever changing in their combinations that come together in my mind. These compose a heaven unique from any other. Never again will these exact things do their dance of existence in such near proximity. The mother with her little girl walks on the deck below. The child bounces a ball, trips for a moment, and the ball goes shooting out of reach into Your Boundless Mercy.

218

Spirit Am I

It is past the bedtime hour and I am up still, listening to the sounds of silence very actively composing this nocturn of ever-present beauty. I hear the refrigerator motor humming its drone. I eat a raw carrot and notice the crunching noise of chewing between my ears. Shifting my focus to sight, I revel in the color and shape of a small fall pumpkin in its various shades of yellow and orange. It is a brilliant burst of brightness on the dark brown depth of a stained oak tabletop. The plane of the wood stretches a few feet into the lurking shadows of night as I sit at one end scratching my ode onto the page. I crunch another small carrot as the writing continues. The motor stops its drone as I notice the deep inhaling from my wife's slumber coming from the room next door. The cycles of life spin on into infinity. I am here in awe of the grandeur before me. Would I not be at the very core of Divine Glory that includes me in this immortal dance of matter? There is always some magnificence to witness and make note; nothing special is needed. Just the very act of seeing is a wonder beyond description. Who could make an eye but God Who gives us holy vision? The all-inclusive goes on forever. Does any but the Son of God have ability to ponder infinity? Does any animal but man perceive a dimension beyond the stars? Spirit am I, a holy Son of God, free of all limits, safe and healed and whole. I am the Son God loves, so therefore do I extend as well this Boundless Mercy.

219

Present in My Joy

There is music in the air, and we are enjoying the cool atmosphere of fall enveloping the afternoon scene down by the river. Not a cloud in the sky, the bright light illuminates the white boats on the water and reflects across the surface of the shimmering stream. We can relax as people walk about and sit at the tables that are scattered around. We can sip our beverages as we appreciate the setting and our natural place in it. The Navy Yard is a vibrant neighborhood now on the shores of the Anacostia, south of Capitol Hill. All is well in this world of exceptional grace. Do the universal forces come forth to the highest place I can be in the flow of creation? I am present in my Joy. I am noticing the all-pervasive presence of the Divine Mother. I am flowing in the genius of masterful inspiration that emanation from God can only provide. I receive and give back in the words of elation. I pause and notice the quiet nature of things. The ivy grows up the wall and creeps over the edge of the concrete crest. There is a festive feeling in the atmosphere coming from the music playing over the loudspeakers. All is enveloped in the general joy of the moment. Helicopters buzz by, flying along the course of the river. Many are relaxing on the long green lawns. A man dressed in black gets up from his chair and walks away, carrying a black backpack. Another man sits cross-legged on the stone steps down below. I come to absorb Your Love in the many forms of this scene of Boundless Mercy.

220

A New Vibration Regardless

We are coming up to an election. Much controversy is in the air and people are divided into camps of "for or against." One can hardly praise the good works of either side without being ostracized by the group of the "other." Who is this "other" we so openly criticize but a major piece of our SELF? So then would all attacks be flagellation of our own being? What is divided upon itself cannot stand tall and rise above the inequities of this world. Rather would this imagined separation from us into tribes disparate and groups of self-righteous preachers of damnation who do not see the potential for great Joy is always present. Great beings have said the "enemy" is not always wrong, and love given to one must be given to the other. We cannot be so certain our agendas work or that any agenda is superior to that response in the moment that is formed from necessity. An election is coming up and the people will decide. We will have a new vibration regardless of this side or that side winning. There will be a loser and a winner. Yet God from every atom of creation spins the quantum physics of Truth through the endless media of this Cosmic neutrality of matter exactly as it is, unaffected by what we think or even do. What blazing present would turn our heads around in a flash? We could not possibly know to elect that state of Being free of all conflict, being still in the sway of opposing forces that battle for ascendancy. Only one place merits our election and that is Yours of Boundless Mercy.

221

I Come to Be

I come to Be not to Do. An intrinsic Action of Life requires no struggle or effort, no exploitation and no labor, no worry or concern for outcomes. The tree that bears apples does not consider the morning dew must be earned, nor would it question the production team about its algorithms that line up the sun and rain and space to be itself. It grows apples regardless of its cares, without calculations about yield or even usage. Who eats the apples is not its concern. Why not myself, greater than a tree of forbearance, rest in that certainty of Being not "doing"? I come to mend the past, yet in that final declaration of a clean bill of health would my divine nature come forth unencumbered. I do not know the way to a better nirvana than this: I am already whole and free on purpose and in every way perfected. What need have I to doubt myself or struggle in the ways of self-improvement? or seek to add to the already created version of myself who God the Father planted on this planet now as me? I need to walk around a bit and wrap my head around this vision. No more "doing" to make some different character of who I really am. This Self I share with God is already fully here, ever amidst my former sleep of forgetfulness. I jot down these lines as I often do with the new beginning of an action that never ceases. I am here to extend Your Love in whatever form I deem fitting. This is my expression of Boundless Mercy.

222

This Rock Remains

At the end of a long cycle, it seems, on what rock of this Mother Earth do I stand expecting that my place here would make a difference to usher in a reality of Boundless Mercy? This rock on which to build that church of the human race is always some absolute version of Divine Love. Does it defy the definition of science? Perhaps. Is it seen in the workings of new algorithms of thought and measurement? I could question it maybe unaware of the extent this new science of predictability has conditioned my daily actions. Yet this rock remains. Long after the dissolution of the human race, if that is where we are going, will be the rock of ages—an orb in the cosmos of infinite orbs. Life goes on in the rock, in the atomic explosion of matter, endless in nature to the far reaches of the unfathomable. These few odes, taking up the attention of my days for a spell, are coming to a natural close. I am here declaring them complete for now. I am pondering my next action of the pen. Upon what bedrock of Your Love will my new attentions rest in these times of the Great Sequester? I am given one place in which to stand and assess the blowing wind of a whole nation, here in this Capitol City on a shining hill of something more than what we think. One cannot unlive history, all the pain and sorrow, yet we can step into the light of a different day. Perhaps one that has not shone its light on the endeavors of humans everywhere before. To this light I sing an endless song of Boundless Mercy.

Epilogue

The Presence of the Divine surrounds all people, places and things. There is no challenging situation that it will not come forth to meet with us, standing before us and behind, to the left and to the right, above us and below, even the deepest despair of doldrums we may find ourselves in life. We need but call and the Mother of the Universe will greet us with a Love beyond measure; the Father of the Heavens will descend upon our request to fill our necessity; the Creator of all things will bestow the Peace that is our birthright to possess in certainty. Brothers and Sisters of the Light, may you continue your journey in Good Will, as you see fit, knowing you will always be met in the end by your Maker with the infinite blessings of Boundless Mercy.

About the Author

Markus Ray received his training in the arts, holding a Bachelor's of Fine Arts Degree in printmaking and drawing from the Cleveland Institute of Art, and a Master's of Fine Arts Degree in painting from the Tyler School of Art, Temple University in Philadelphia, PA, USA. Also a writer and a poet, he brings spirituality and sensuality together in these mediums of expression. He is the author of a major work, *Odes To The Divine Mother*, which contains 365 prose poems in praise of the Divine Feminine Energy. Along with the Odes are his paintings and images of the Divine Mother created around the world in his mission with Sondra Ray.

Markus is a presenter of the profound modern psychological / spiritual scripture, *A Course In Miracles*. He studied with his Master, Tara Singh, for 17 years, in order to experience its truth directly. His spiritual quest has taken him to India many times with Tara Singh and Sondra Ray, where Muniraj, Babaji's foremost disciple, gave him the name Man Mohan, "The Poet who steals the hearts of the people." In all of his paintings, writings and lectures, Markus creates a quiet atmosphere of peace and clarity that is an invitation to go deeper into the realms of inner stillness, silence and beauty. He teaches, writes and paints alongside of Sondra Ray, and many have been touched by their demonstration of a holy relationship in action. His iconic paintings of the Masters can be viewed on www.MarkusRay.com which he often creates while his twin flame, Sondra Ray, is lecturing in seminars. Read his essays on Art Look: An Art Lover's Companion on his website.

Markus also gives commentaries and lectures on *A Course in Miracles* in live seminars with Sondra Ray and in his Miracles for You program. You can also hear his Podcasts on *ACIM* here: bit.ly/PodcastACIM.

BABAJI, JESUS & THE DIVINE MOTHER

Sondra Ray & Markus Ray are brought together by the grace of their Master, Maha Avatar Herakhan Babaji. Babaji Himself said, "Markus is my Humbleness. Sondra is my Voice. Together they are my Love." As Ambassadors for Him, their mission is to bring His teaching of "Truth, Simplicity, Love and Service to Mankind" along with the presence of the Divine Mother to the world. They do so through seminars like the New LRT®, the healing practice of Liberation Breathing®, and the study of *A Course in Miracles*. They are unfolding the plan of Babaji, Jesus and the Divine Mother, Who provide a spiritual foundation for their worldwide mission of service. Their relationship is a shining example of what is possible through deep ease and no conflict. They can take you to higher realms of being, where Spiritual Intimacy©, miracles, and holy relationships can become a big part of everyday life. Their major book on relationships they wrote together is *Spiritual Intimacy: What You Really Want With A Mate.* They offer private Liberation Breathing sessions over Zoom and in person, as well as various Seminars and Sacred Quests around the world. They work with Liberation Breathing® to help people free themselves from limiting beliefs and negative thoughts. Their books, seminars and LB sessions encourage people to discover more profound levels of *DIVINE PRESENCE* in their lives, and awaken more awareness of Immortal Love, Peace and Joy in their hearts.

Resources

The work of Markus Ray can be viewed on "Art Look—an art lover's companion." His Website is here: www.markusray.com You can also contact him there on that site, and sign up for his Art Look newsletter.

You can find Markus Ray's books on his Amazon Author's portal here: www.bit.ly/MarkusRay

Markus shares lectures, videos and commentary on *A Course in Miracles* with subscribers to "Miracles for You—1-Year Support Network" You can subscribe here: www.bit.ly/Miracles4You Listen to his Podcast here: www.bit.ly/PodcastACIM

Markus has a Facebook page at:
www.facebook.com/markus.ray.169

You can reach Markus directly at:
markus@markusray.com

Twitter: www.twitter.com/markusray1008

Instagram: www.instagram.com/markusray1008

To Have a Liberation Breathing Session or consultation with Sondra Ray & Markus Ray, book one here: www.bit.ly/LBSession

MARKUS RAY'S Author's Portal :

Bit.ly/MarkusRay

SONDRA RAY'S Author's Portal :

Bit.ly/SondraRay

NOTES

NOTES

Printed in Great Britain
by Amazon

56071838R00147